InspireColor

PATTERNS AND QUOTES FOR TEEN AND ADULT COLORING

By Harper Quinn

Legal Notice:

All rights reserved. This book may not be copied or duplicated for resale or commercial purpose in whole or in part via any means including electronic forms of duplication.

Welcome to "InspireColor:
Patterns and Quotes for Teen and Adult Coloring"!

Within these pages lies a world of artistic exploration and personal growth, where vibrant patterns intertwine with uplifting quotes to ignite your imagination and nourish your soul. As you embark on this coloring journey, I invite you to embrace the transformative power of creativity and self-expression.

Coloring is more than just filling in shapes; it's a canvas for self-discovery and artistic freedom. Each intricate design in this book is a blank slate, waiting for your unique touch to breathe life into it. Whether you're an experienced colorist or just discovering the joys of coloring, let these pages be your playground, where you can flex your artsy skills and unleash your creativity without inhibition.

But coloring is not just about creating pretty pictures; it's about cultivating a positive mindset and uplifting your spirit. Embedded within these patterns are words of encouragement and empowerment, reminding you of your inner strength and resilience. With each stroke of color, let these affirmations seep into your consciousness, boosting your confidence and reinforcing a belief in your limitless potential.

In a world filled with noise and chaos, coloring offers a sanctuary of tranquility and mindfulness. It's a moment of respite from the hustle and bustle of everyday life, where you can immerse yourself in the present moment and reconnect with your inner self. So take a deep breath, pick up your favorite coloring tools, and let the colors flow freely, infusing each design with your unique energy and personality.

What's more, you can create a single picture from each sheet. Whether you prefer to tear out your completed masterpiece for display or keep it within the book as a treasured keepsake, the choice is yours.

As you embark on this coloring adventure, may you find joy in the process, strength in your creativity, and inspiration in the beauty that surrounds you. Let "InspireColor" be your companion on the path to self-discovery and empowerment, reminding you that every stroke of color is a testament to your strength, resilience, and capacity for transformation.

Happy coloring!

Harper Quinn

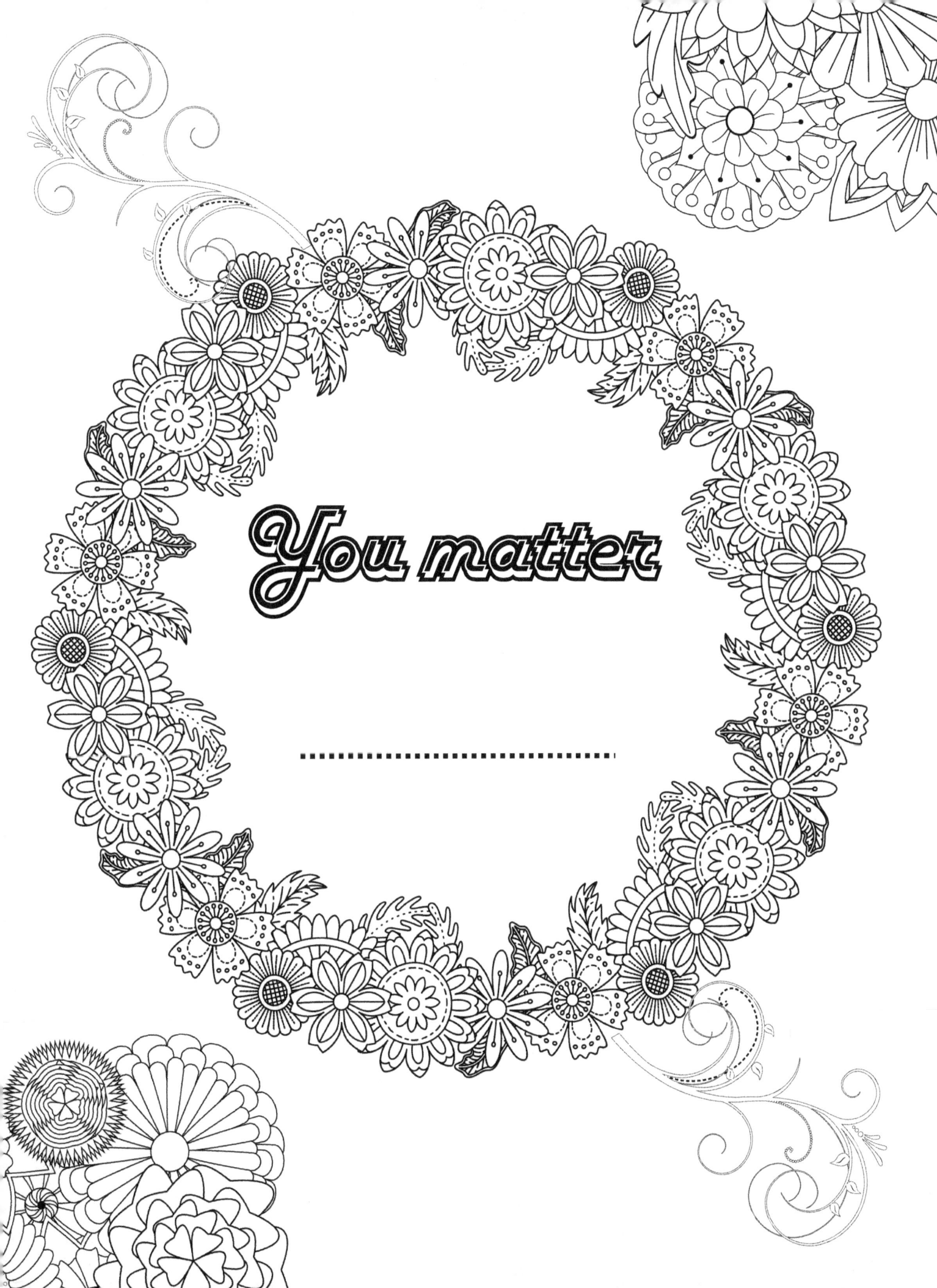

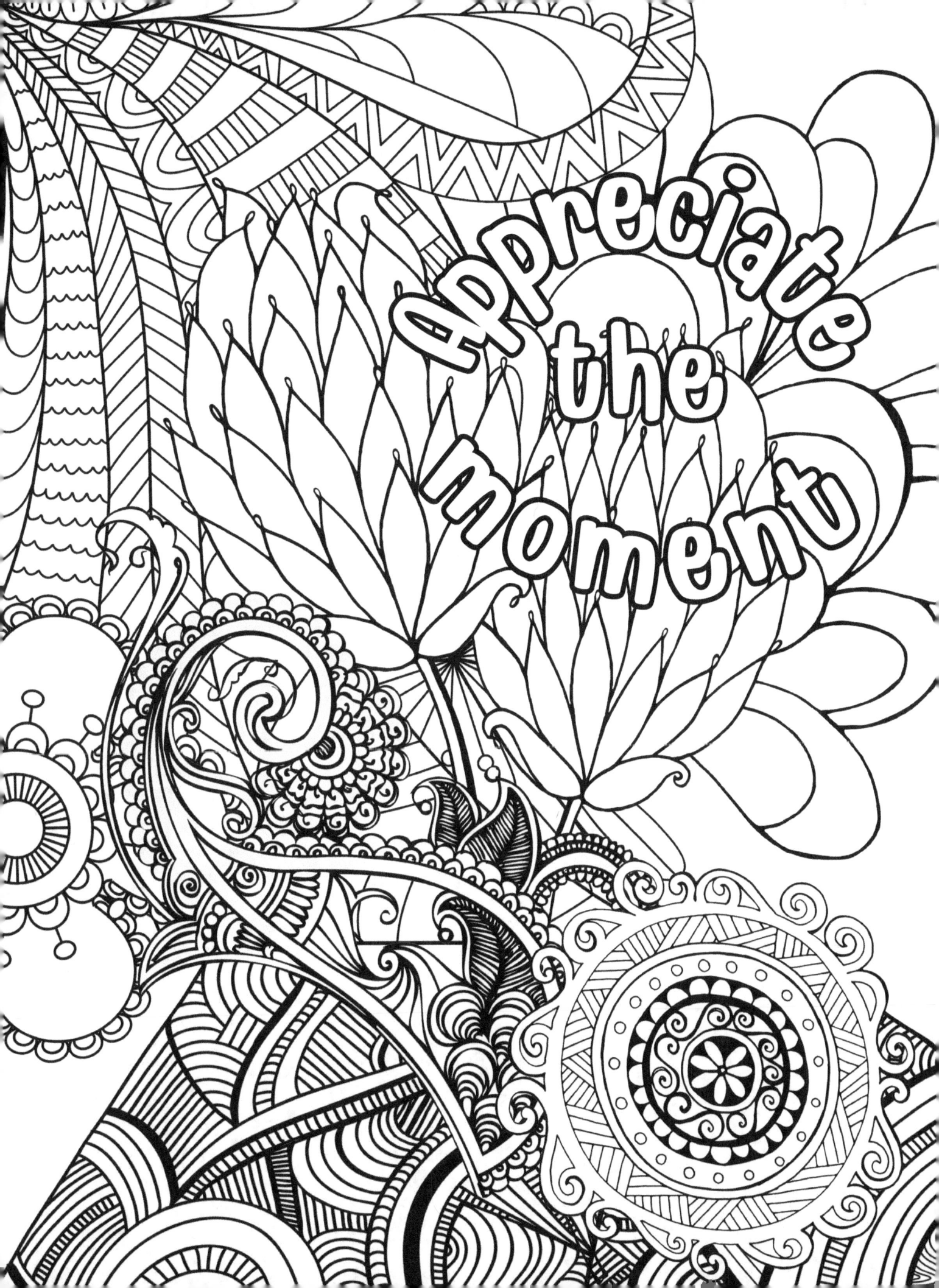

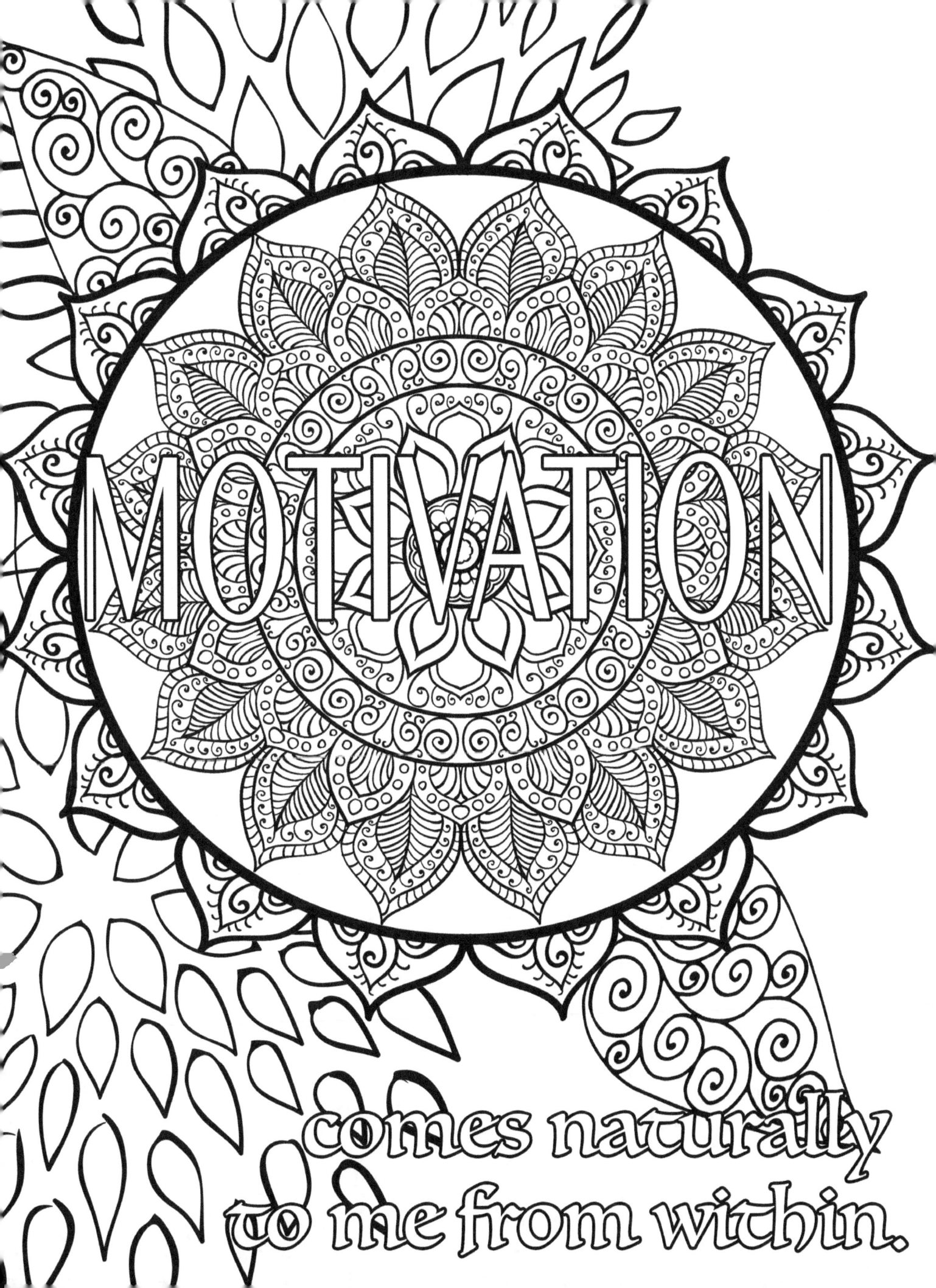

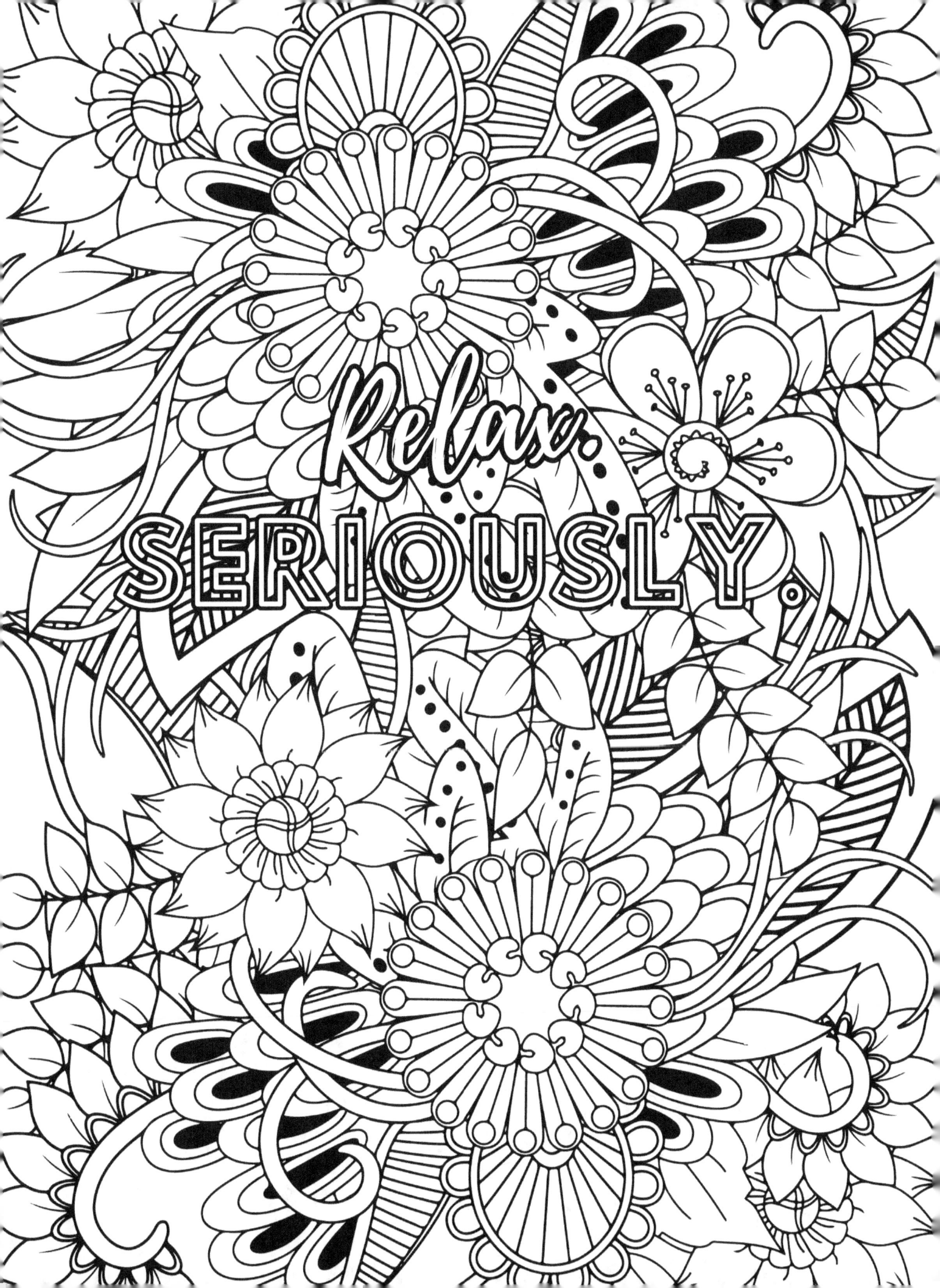

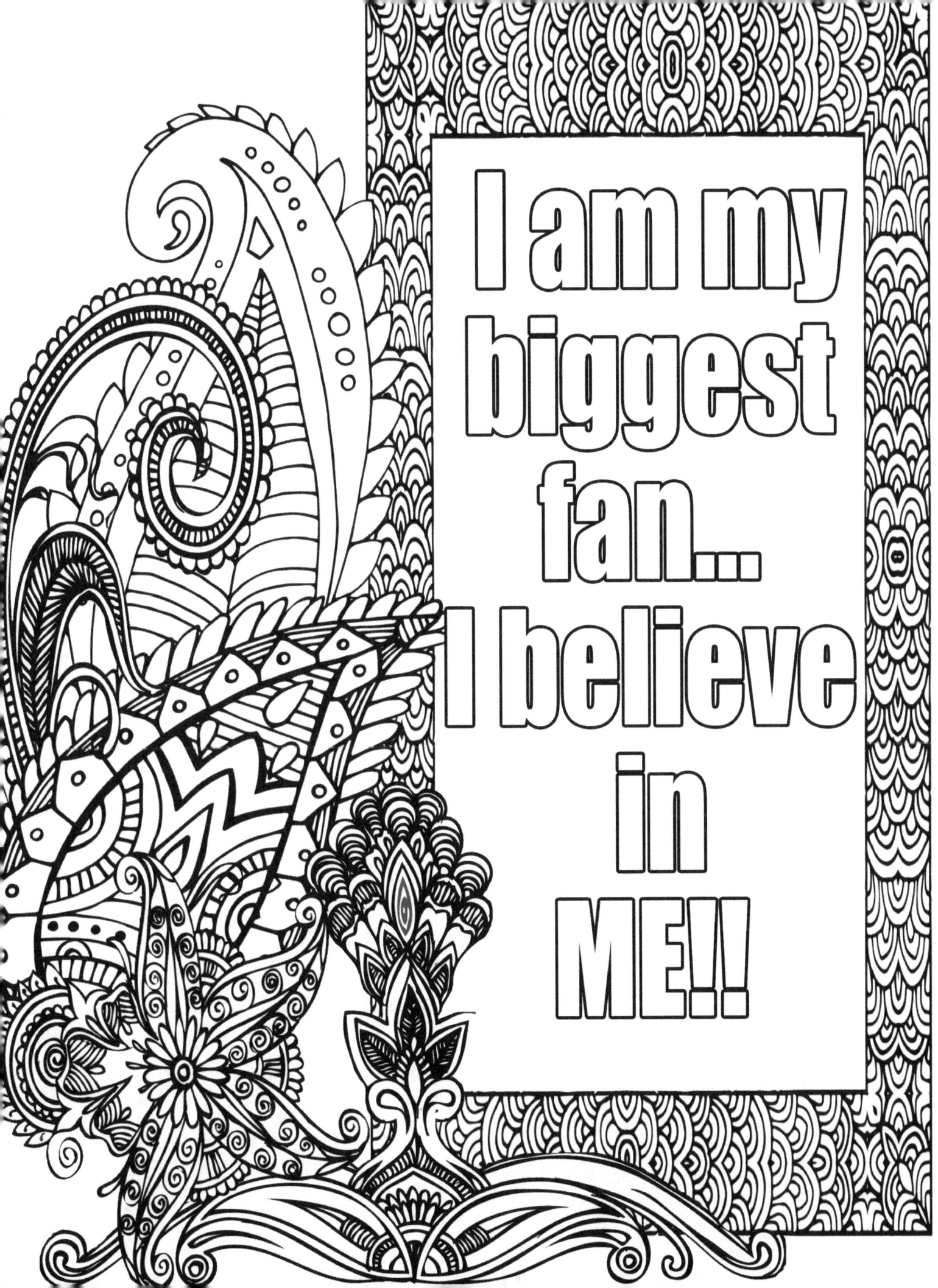

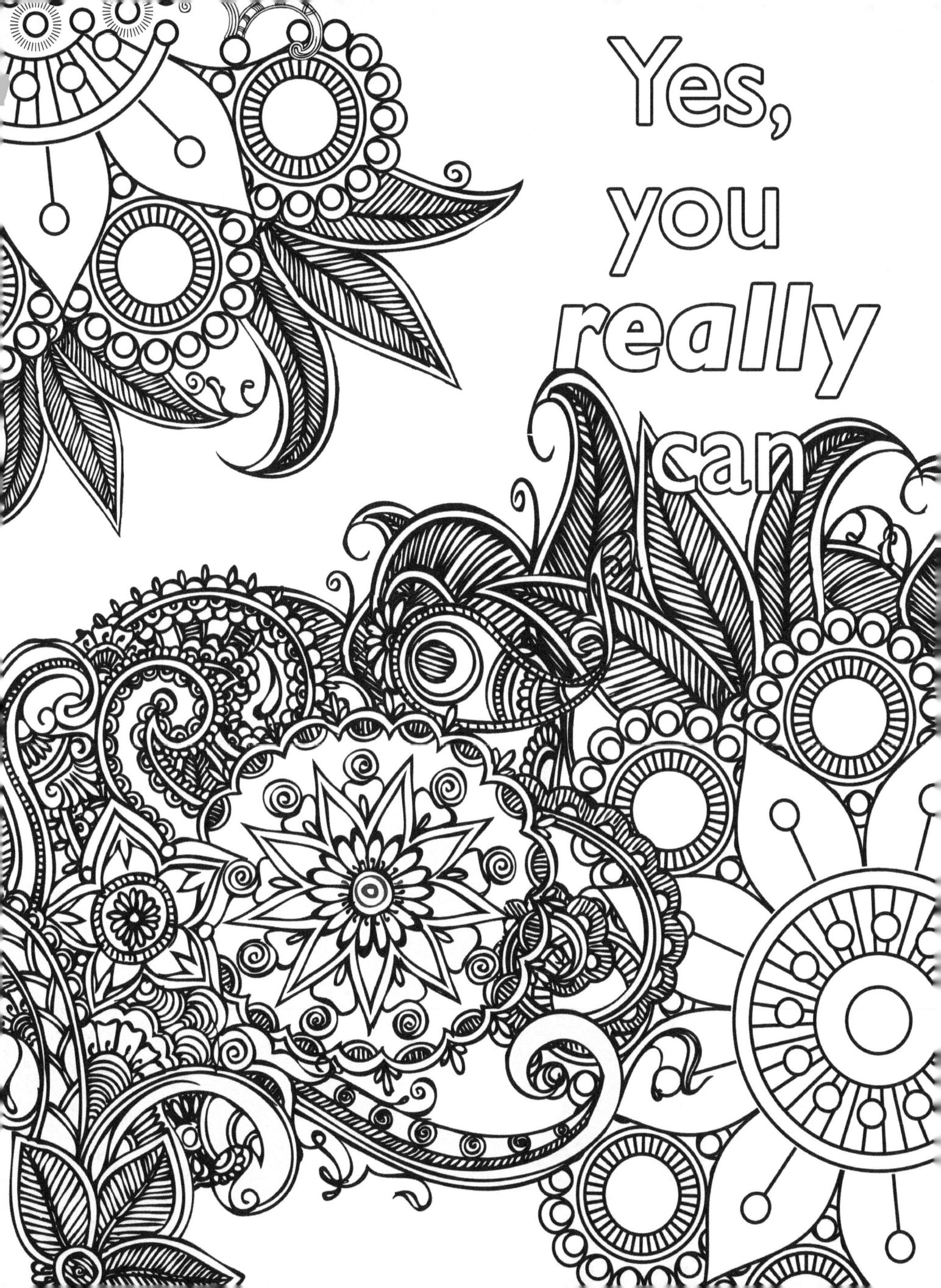

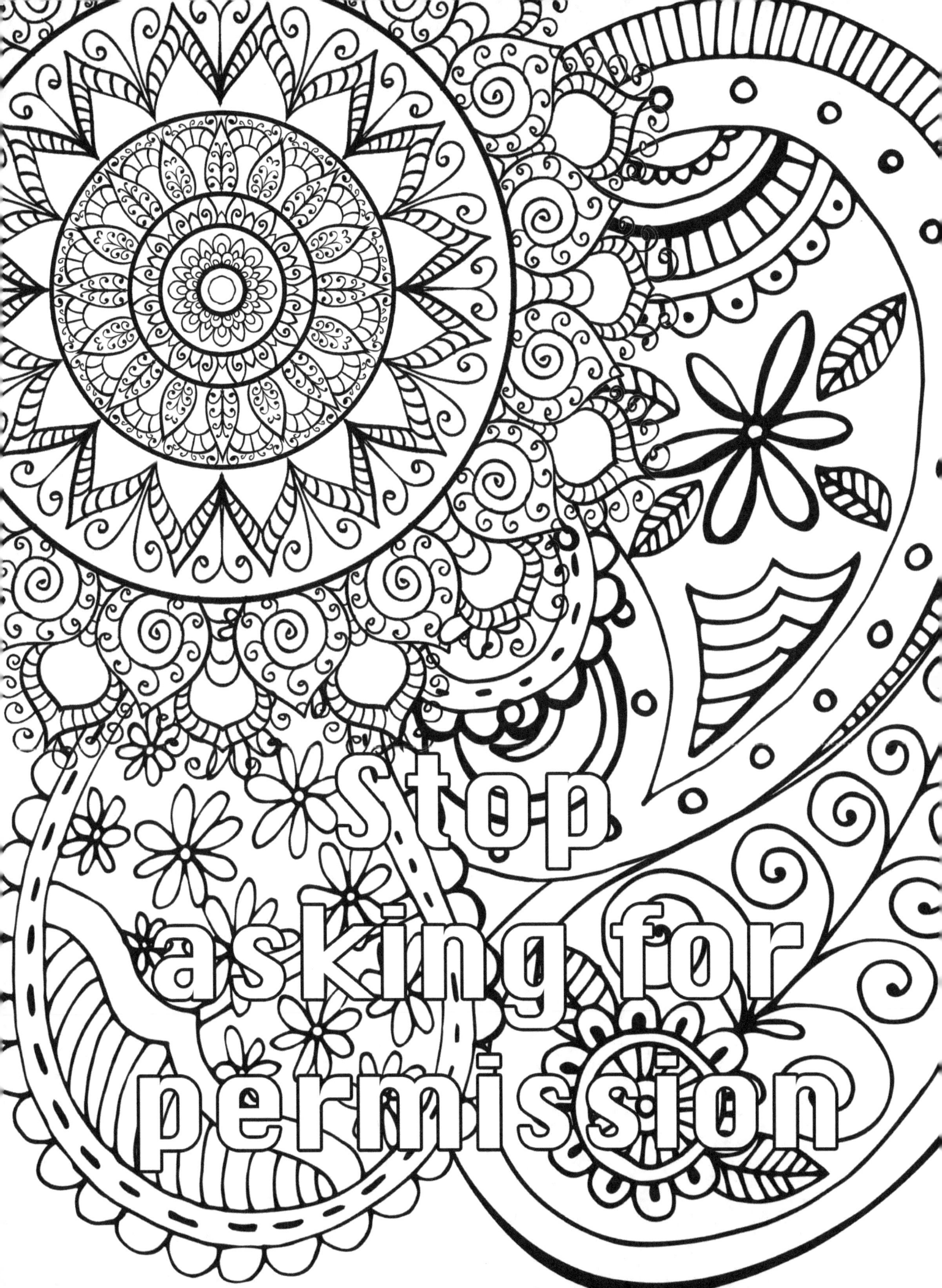

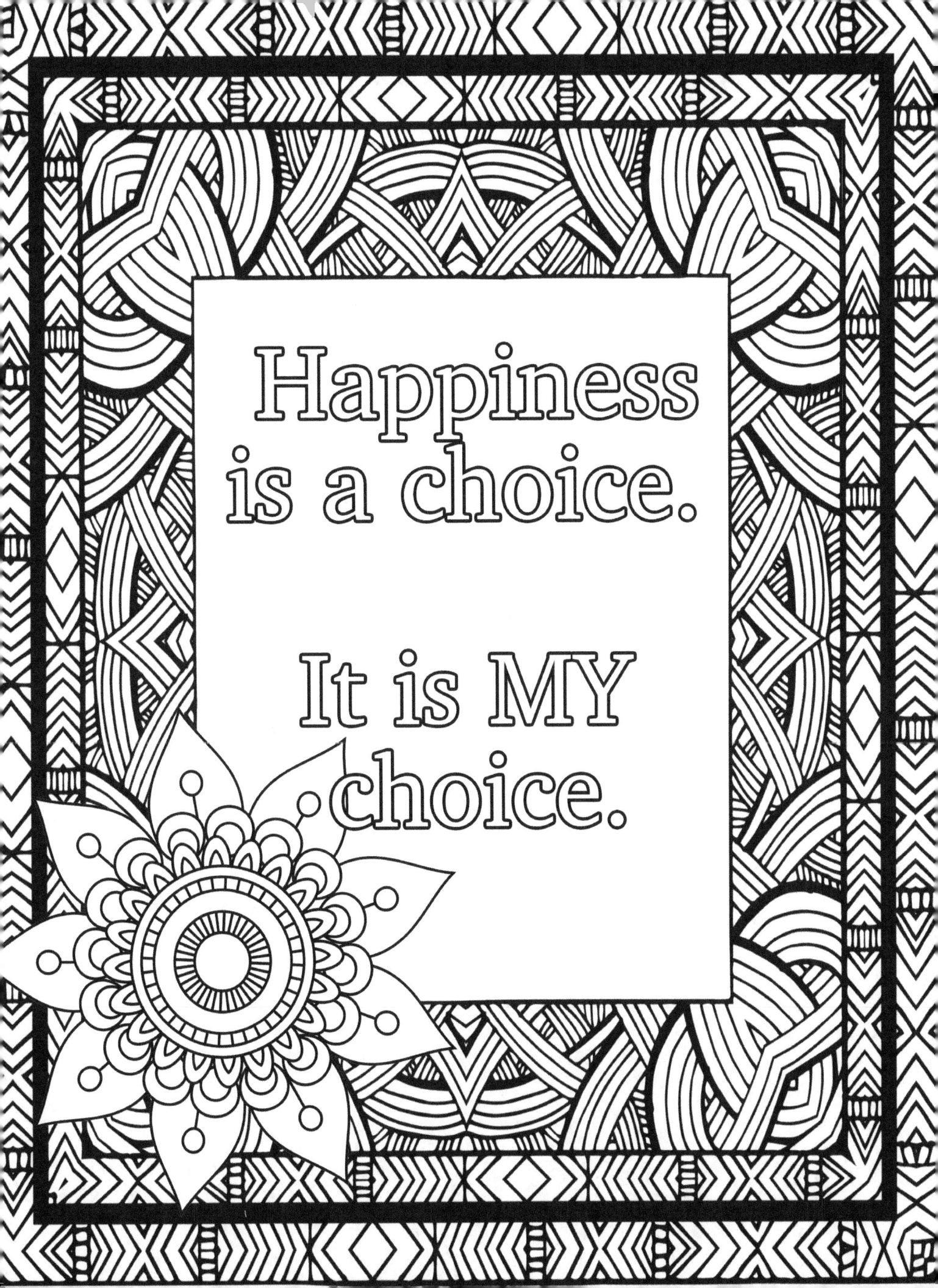

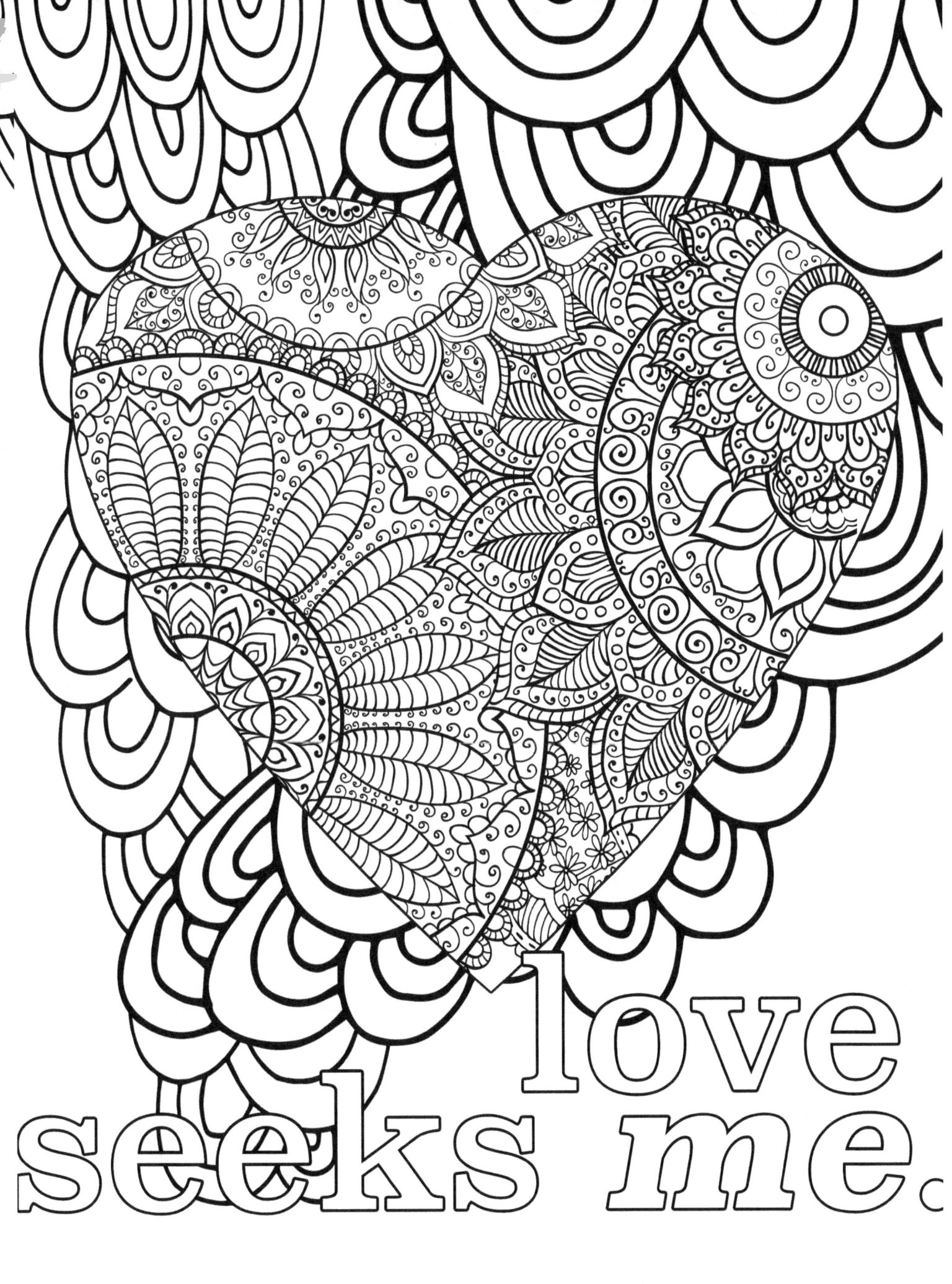

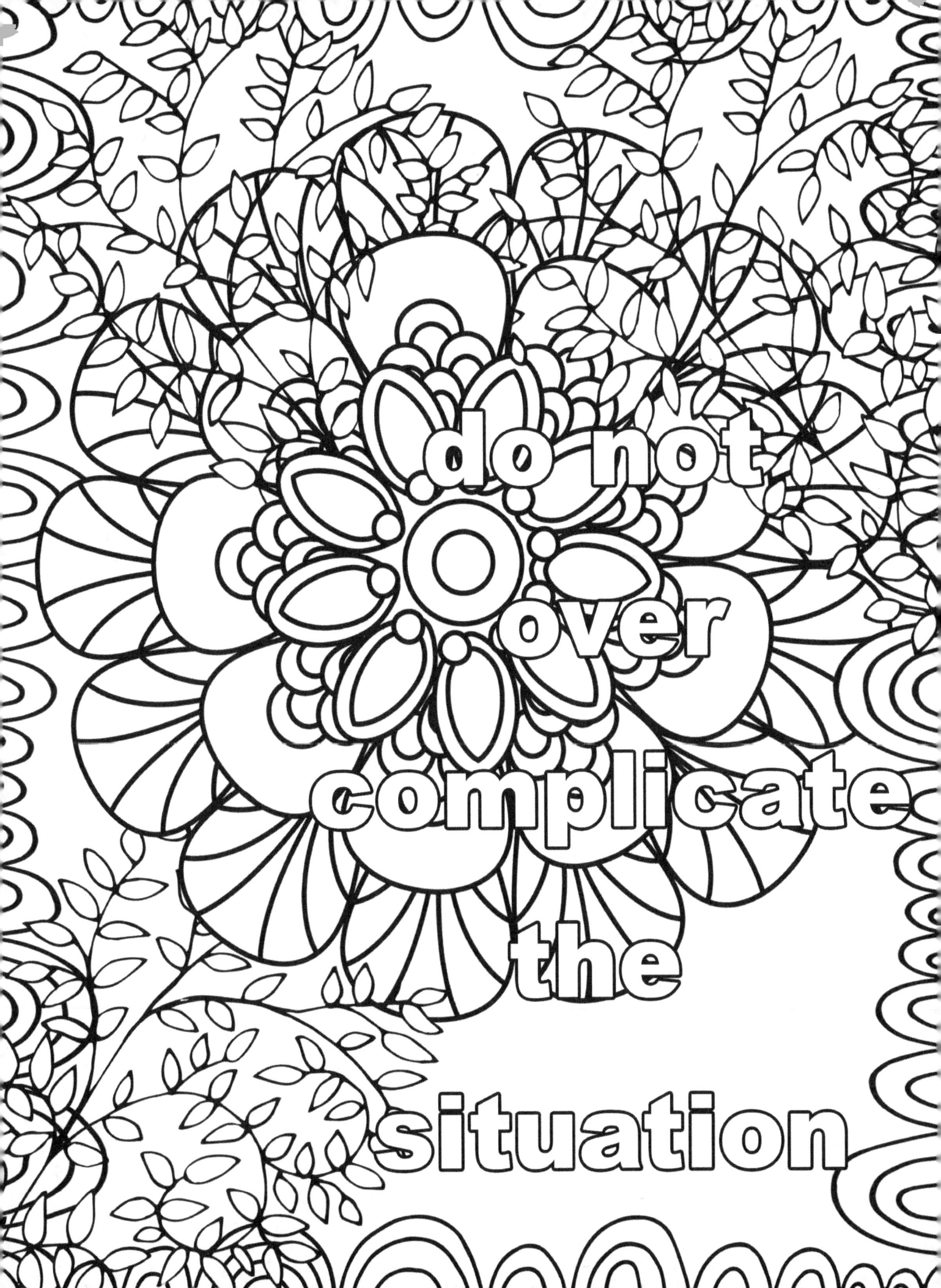

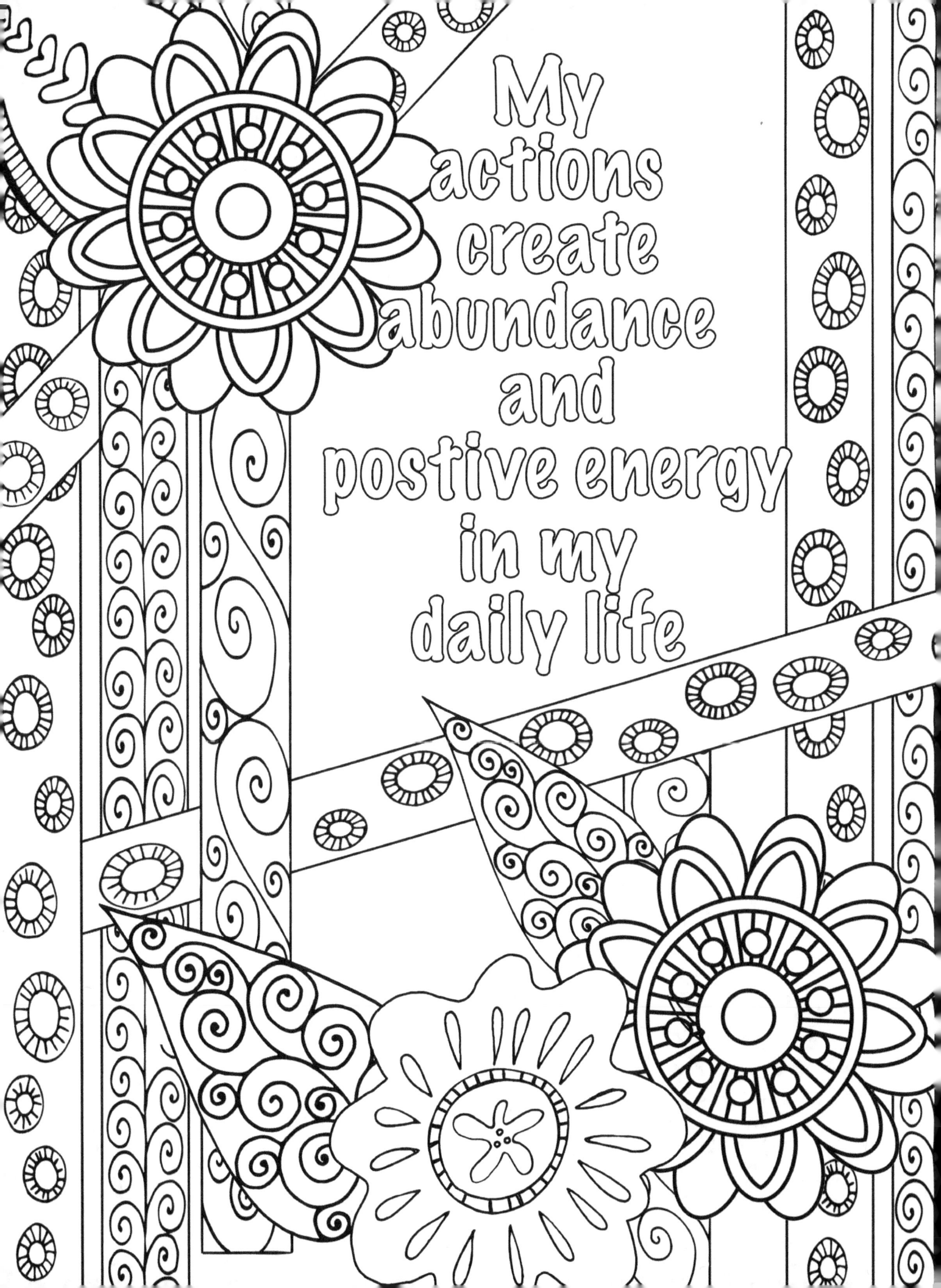

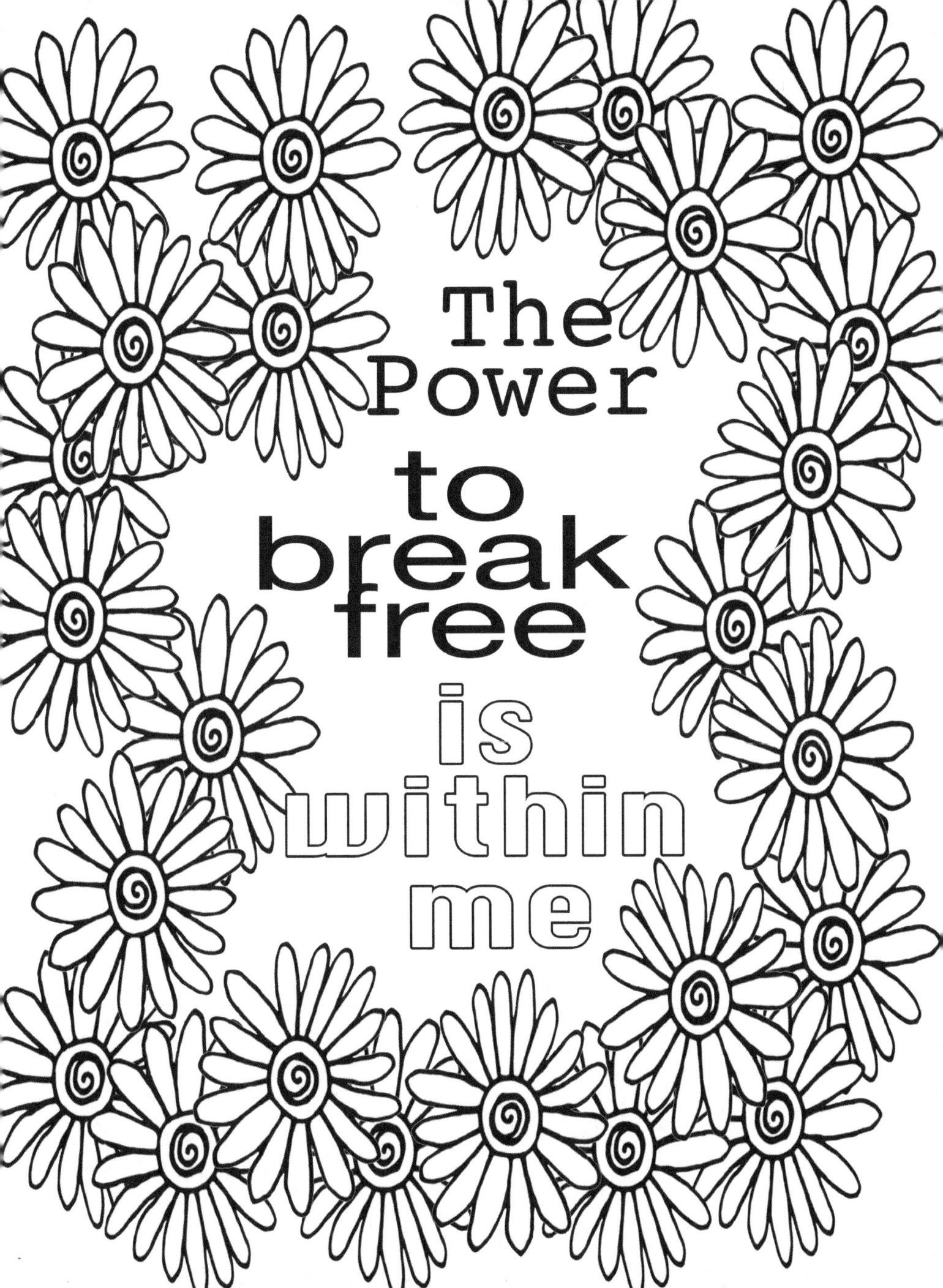

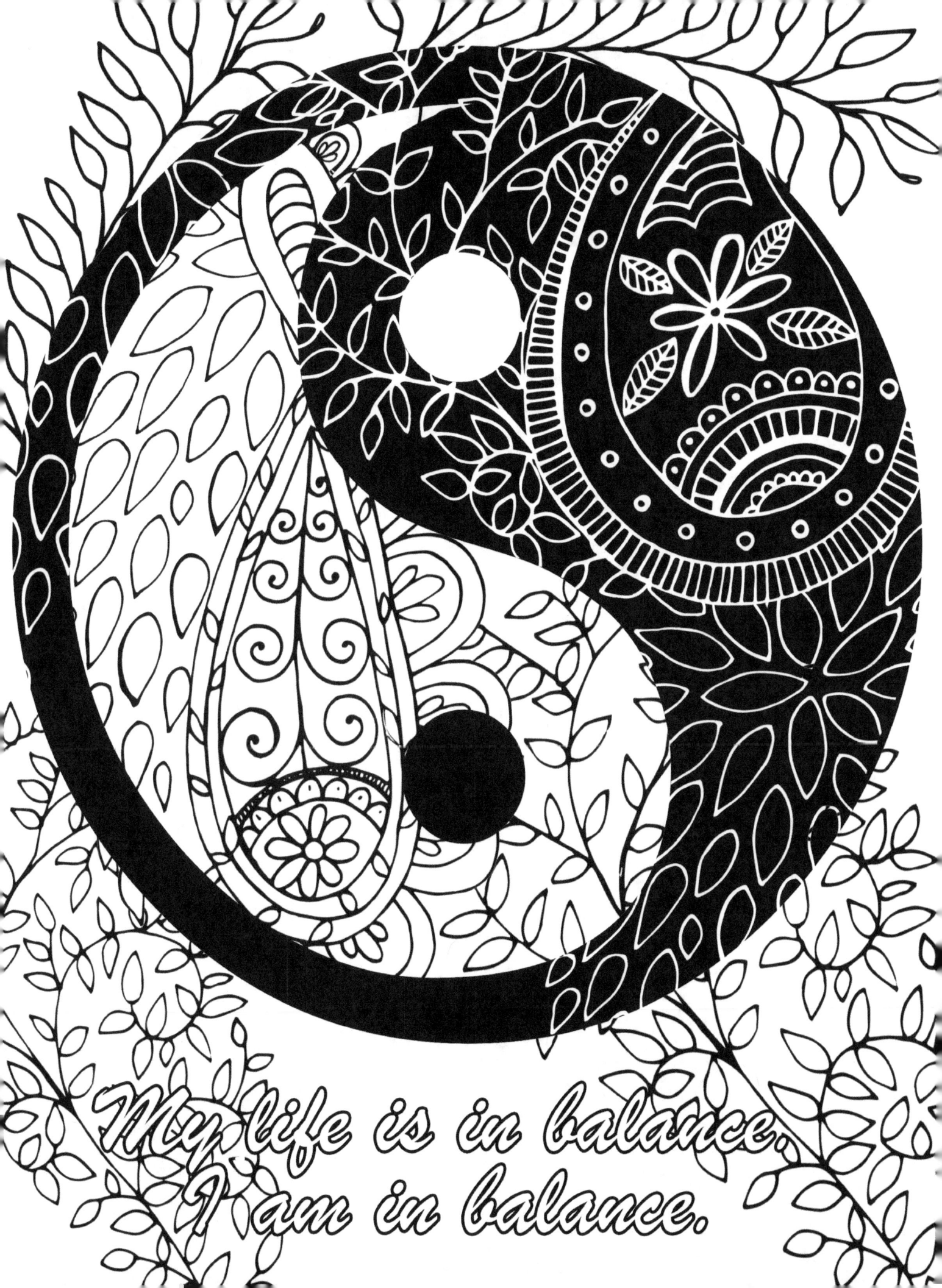

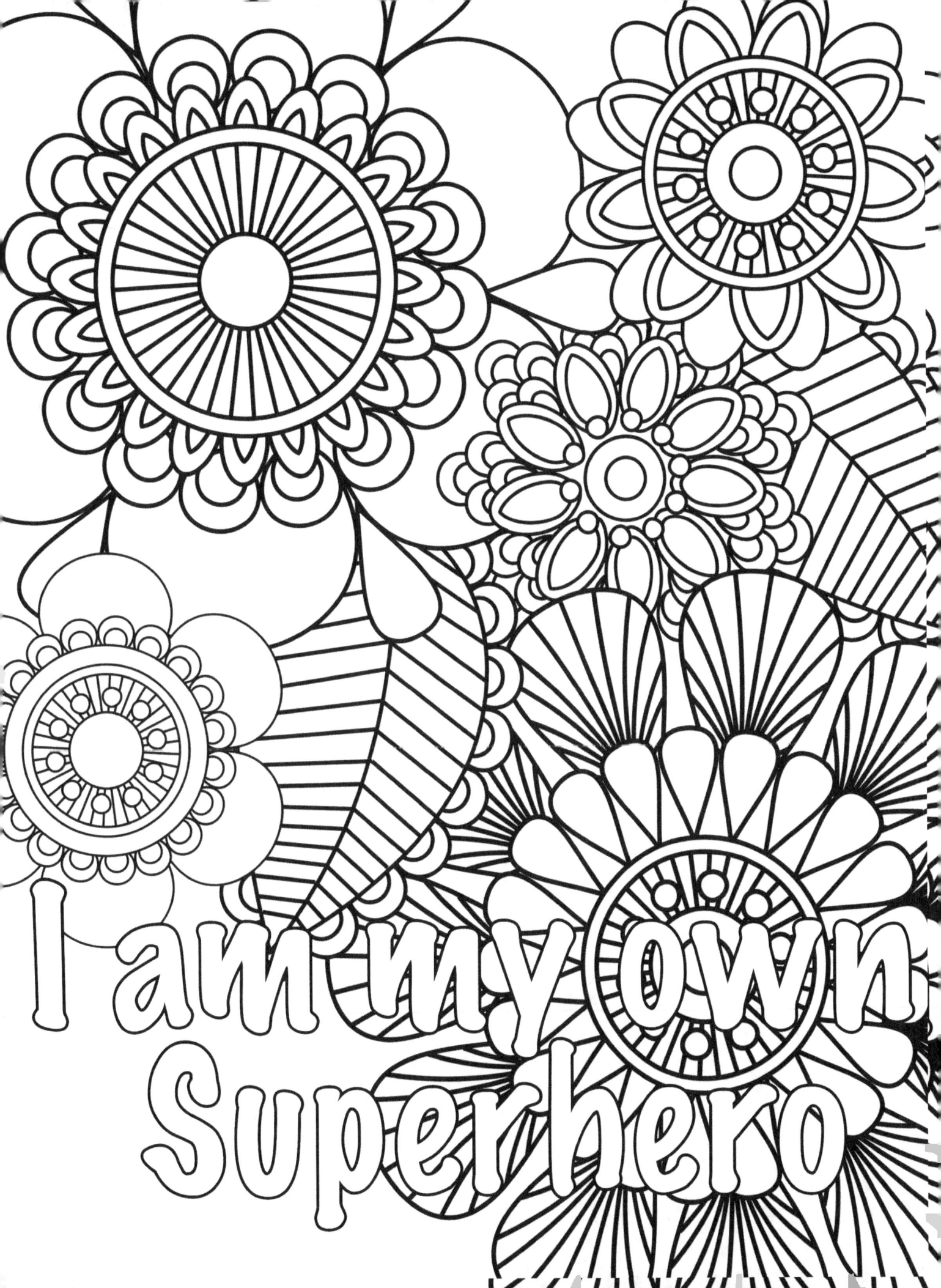

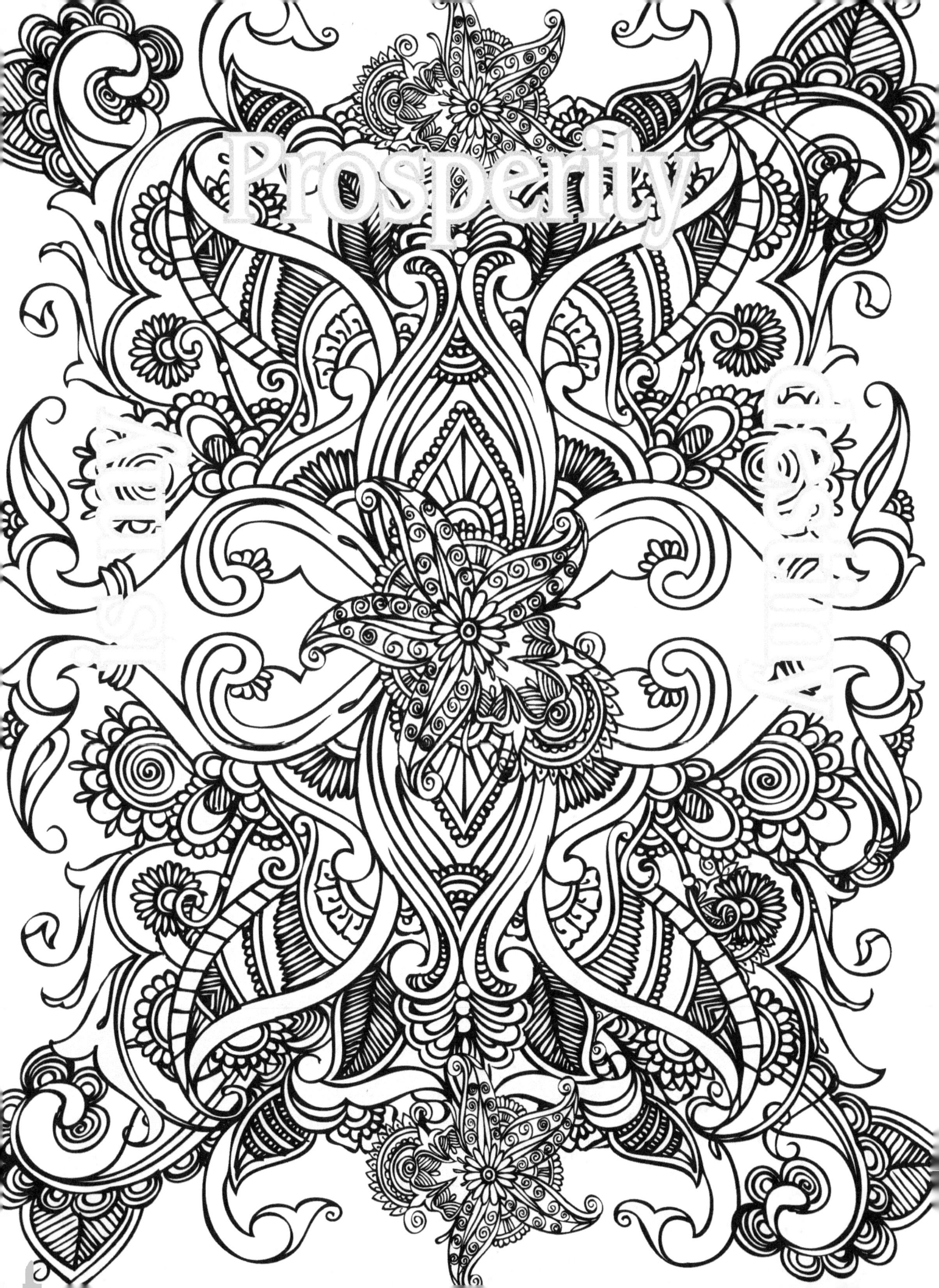

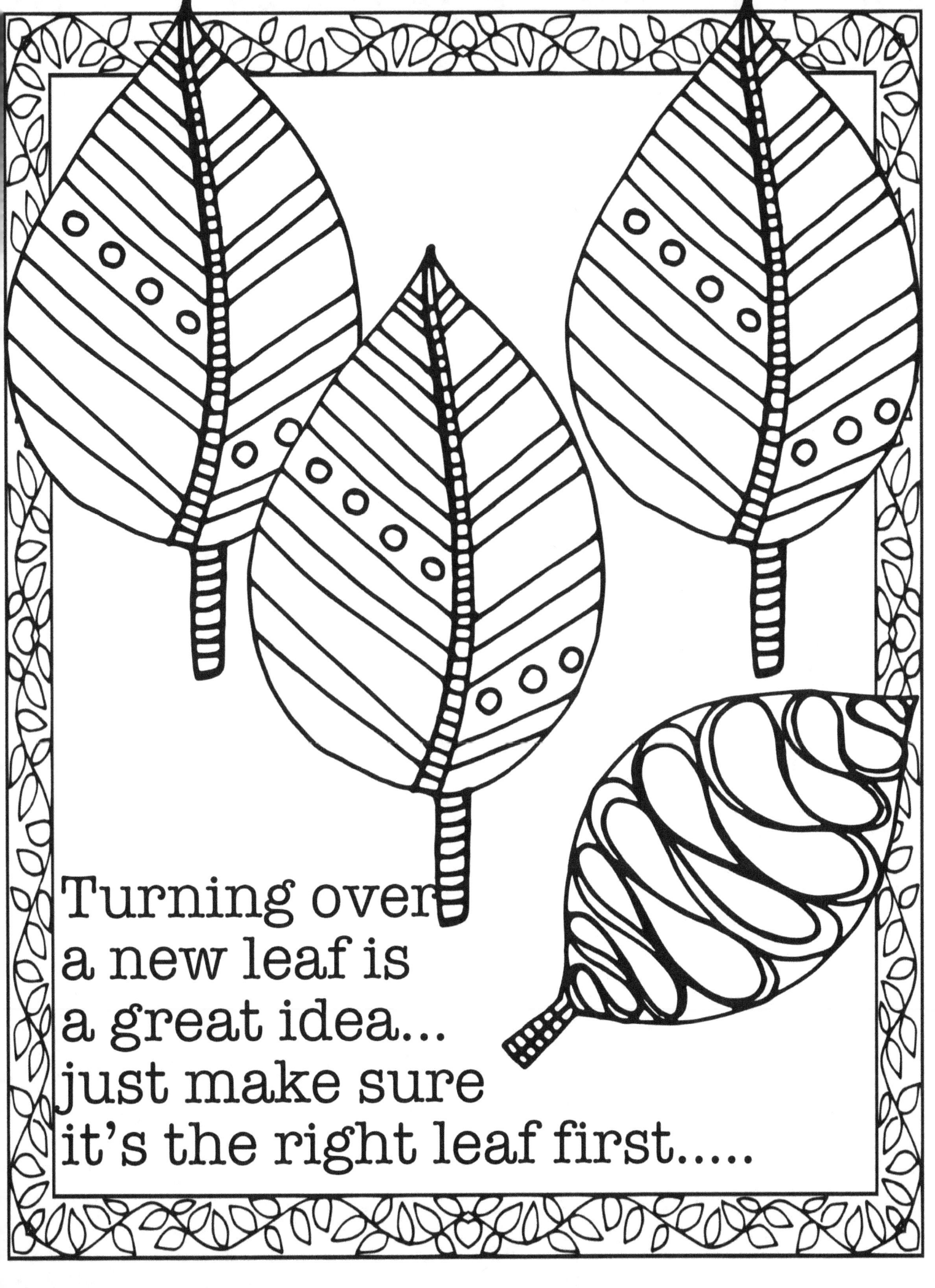

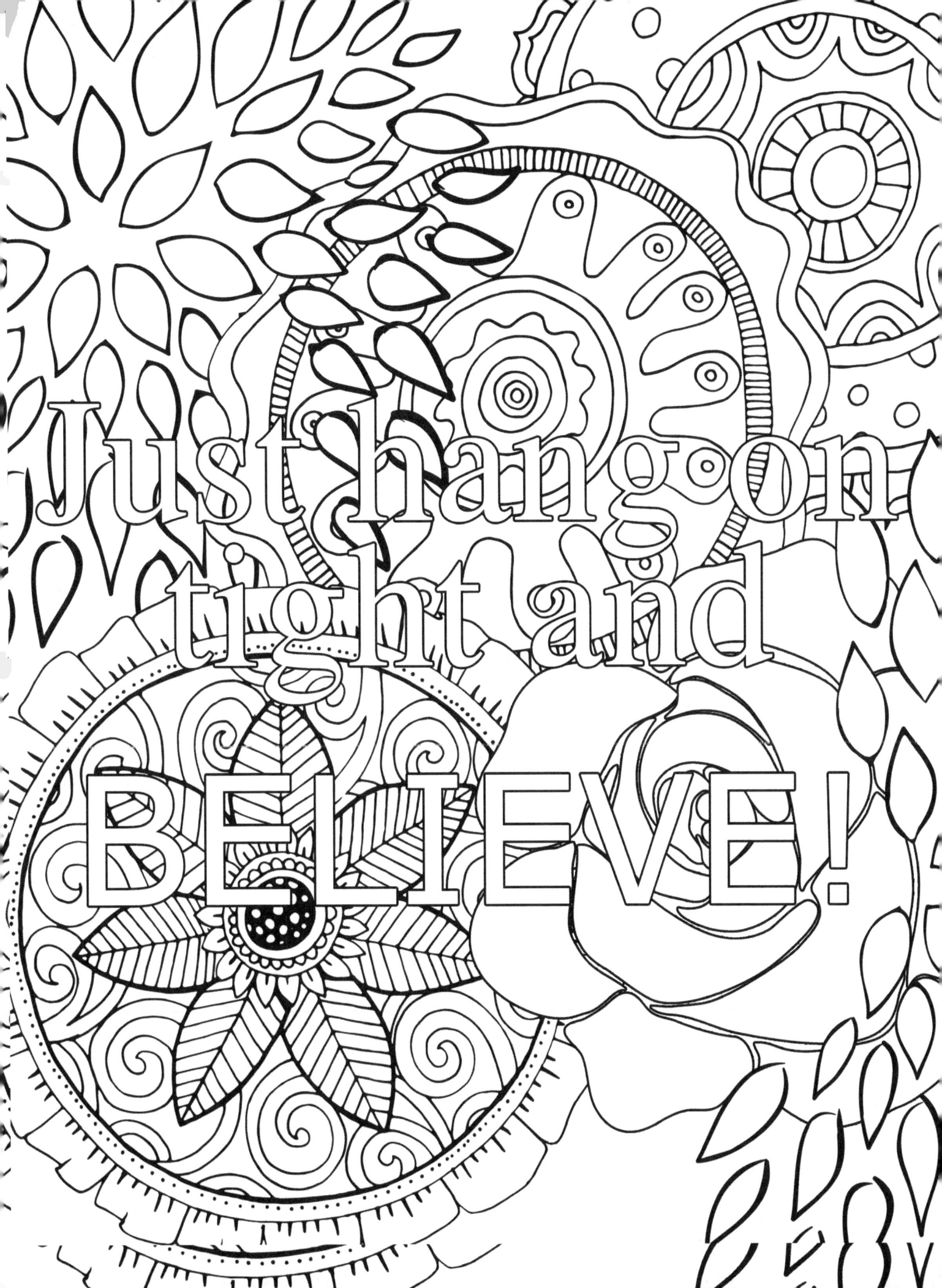

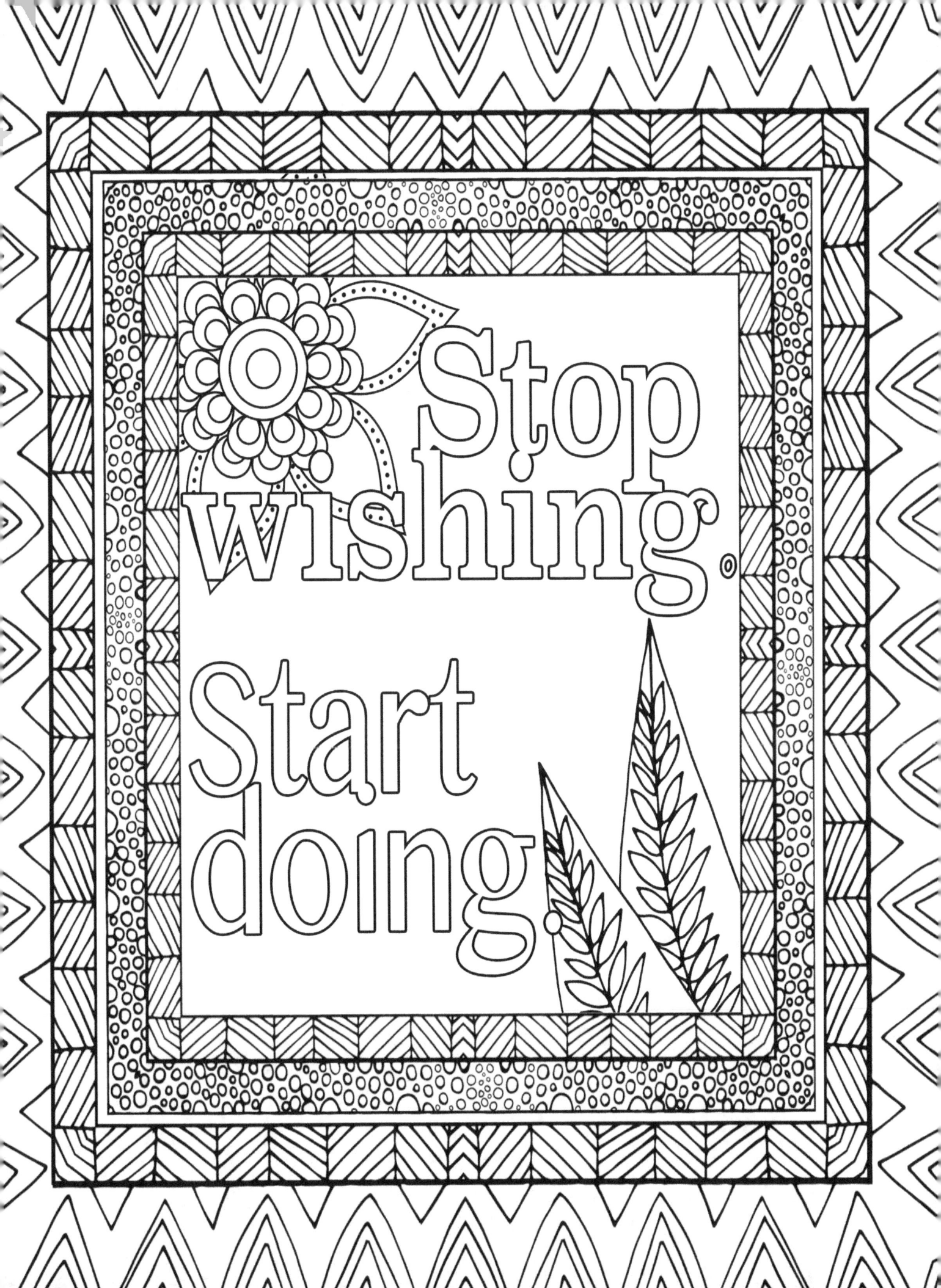

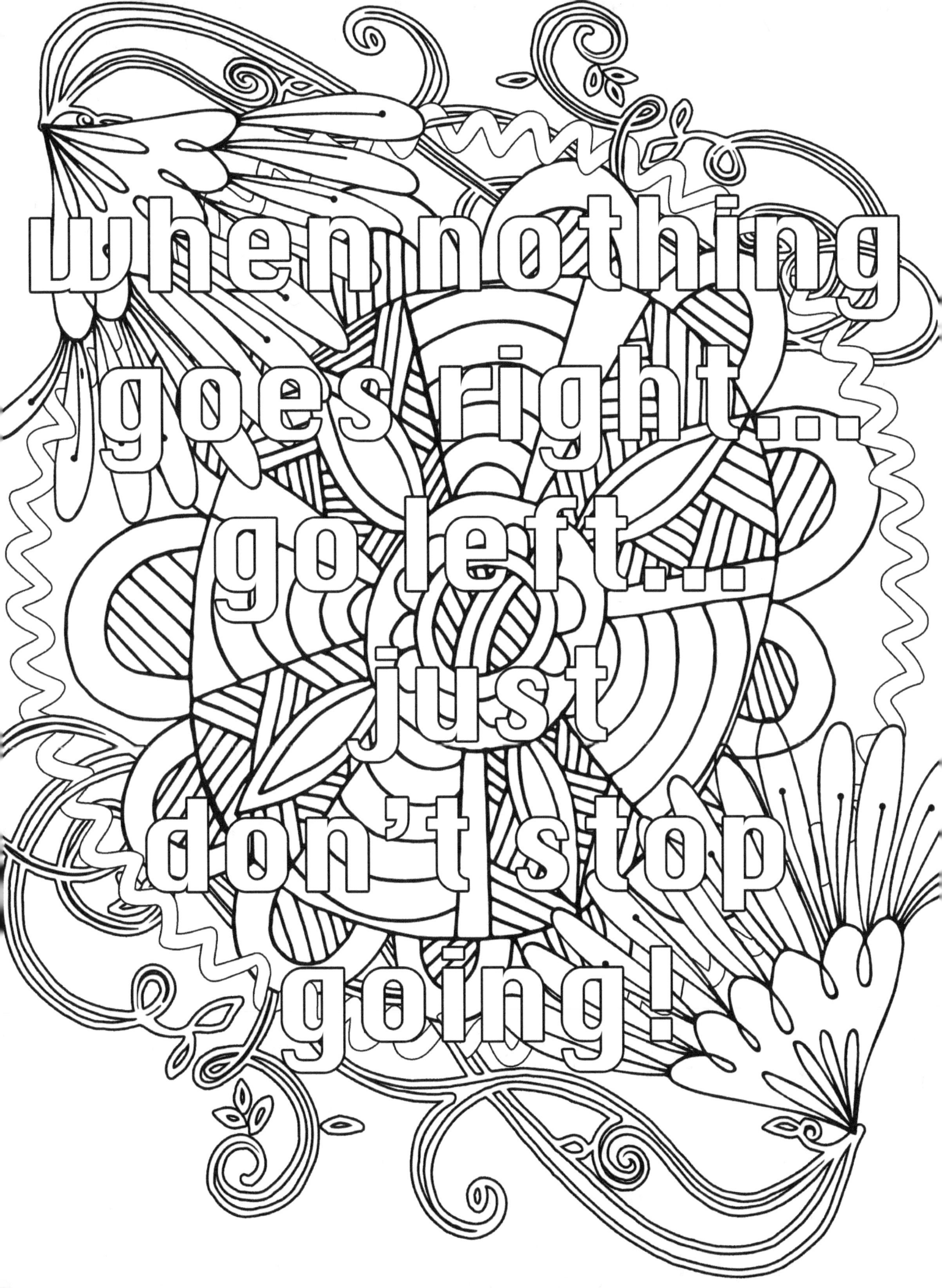

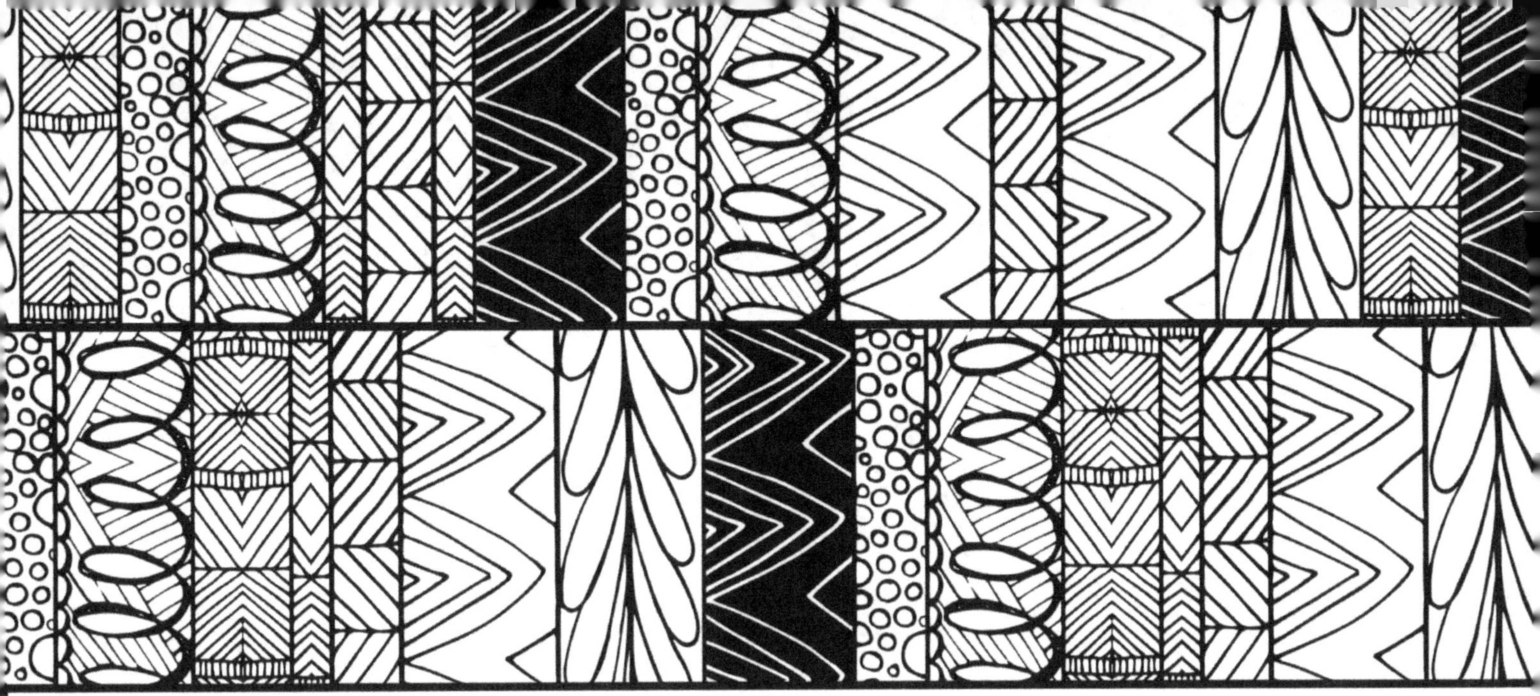

Do what you love.

LIFE IS TOO SHORT TO WASTE TIME ON ANYTHING ELSE.

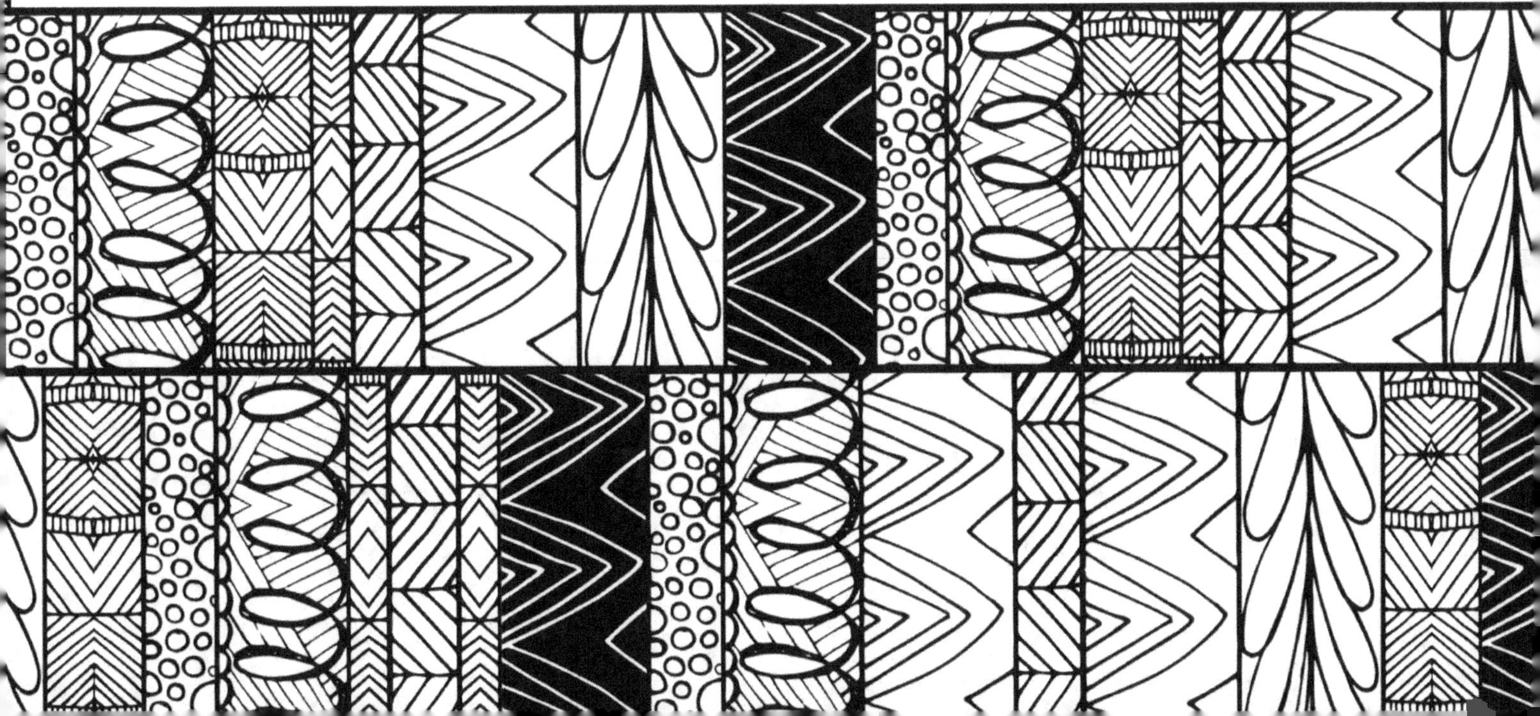

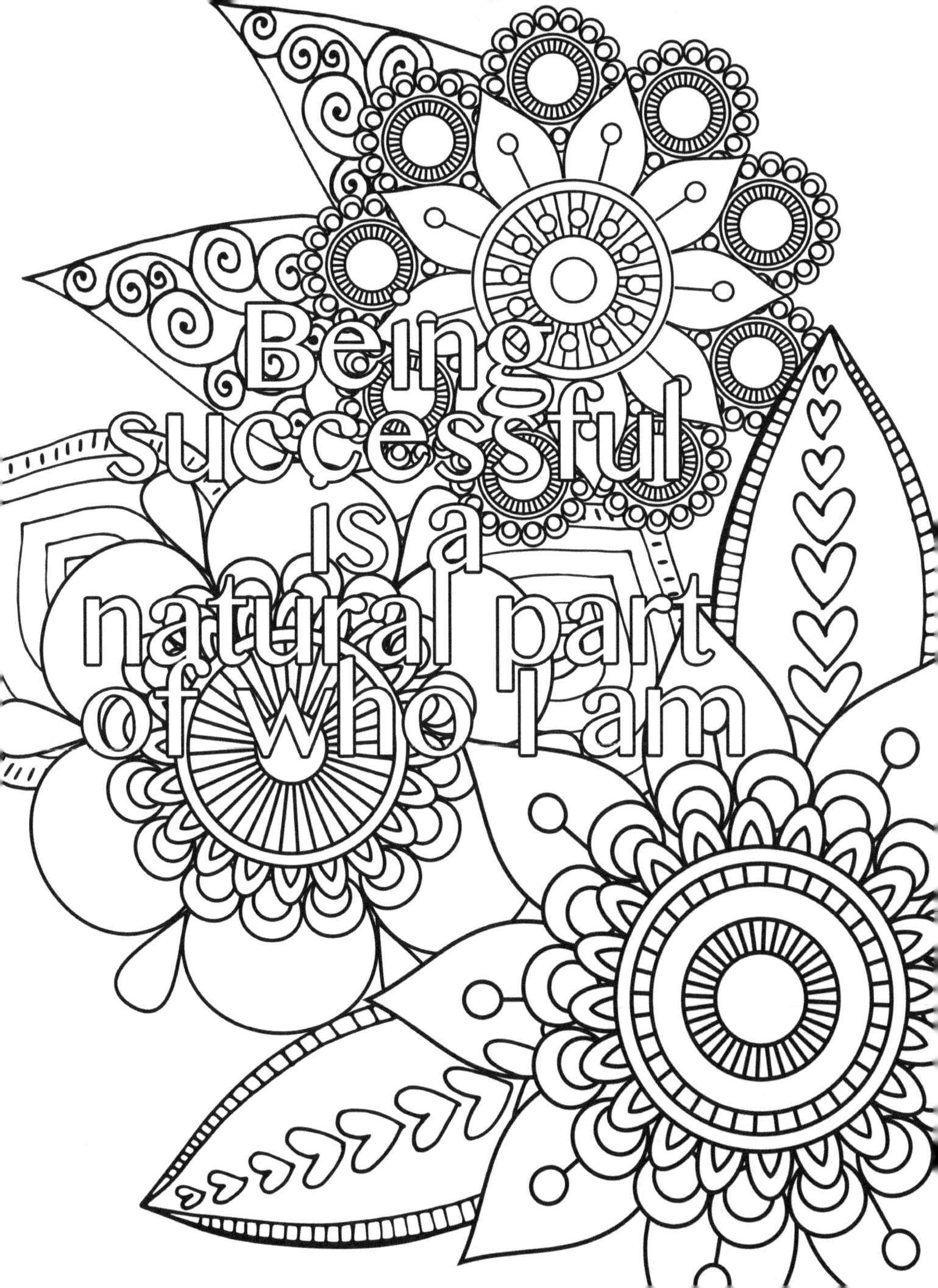

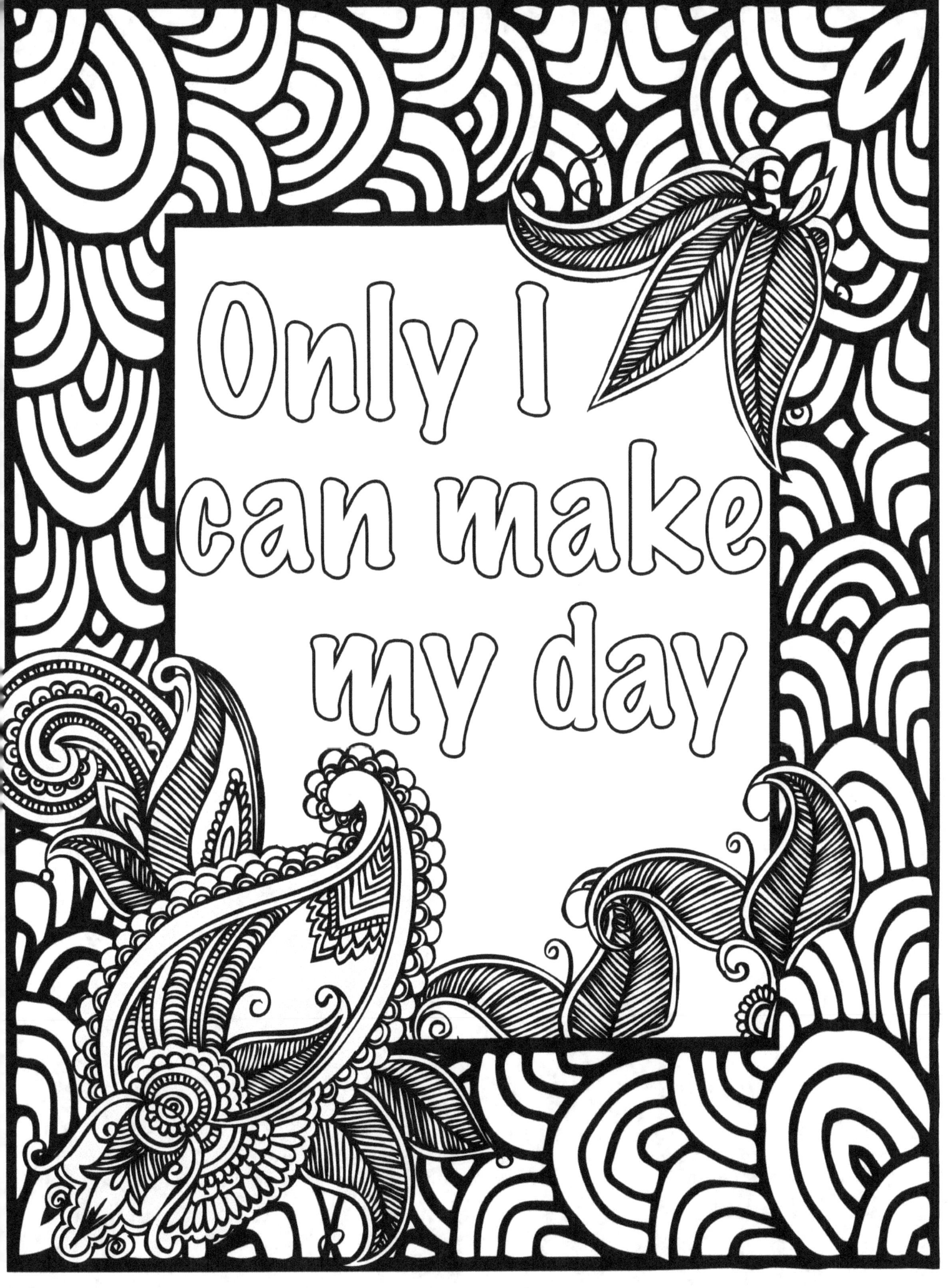

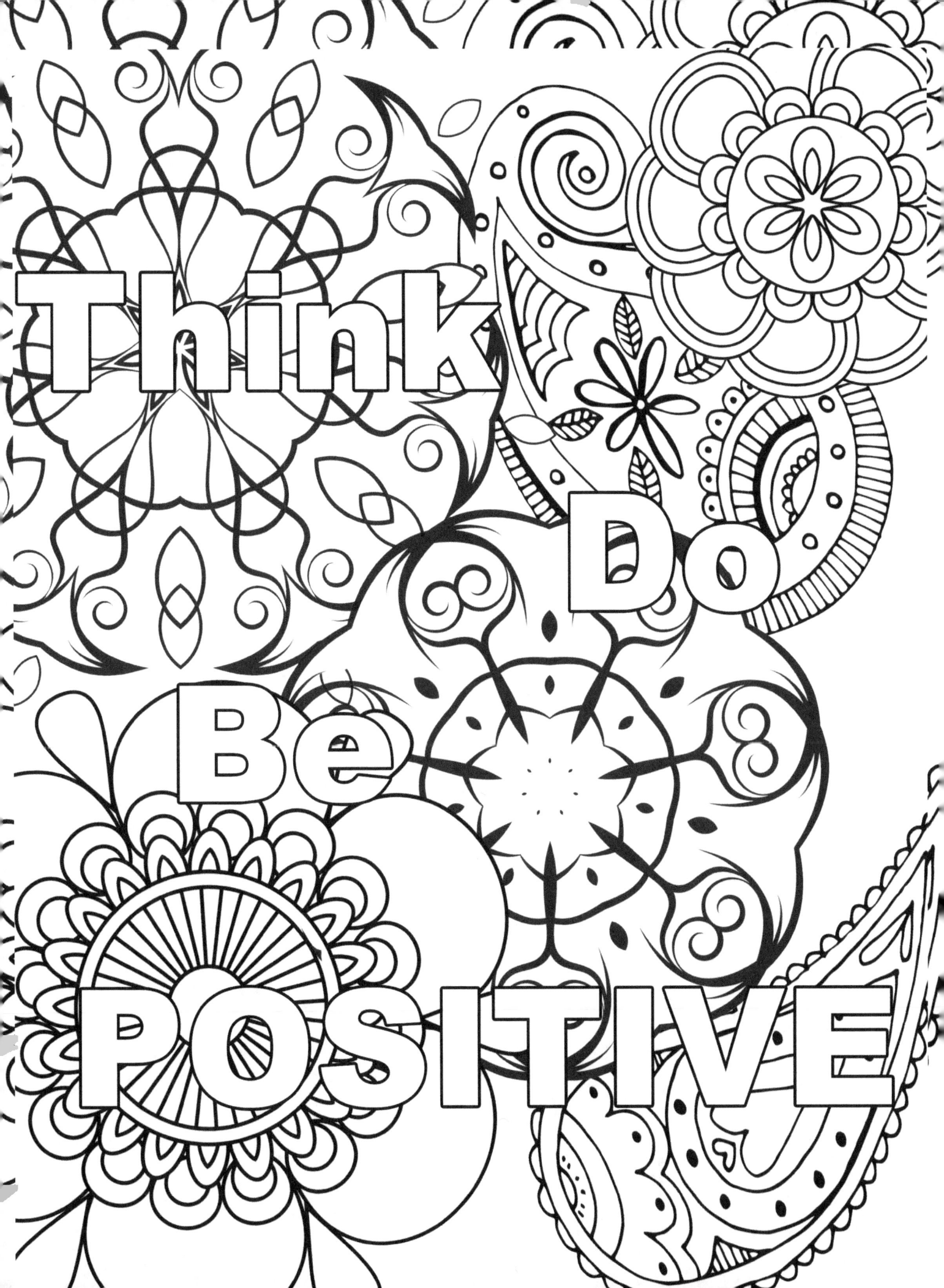

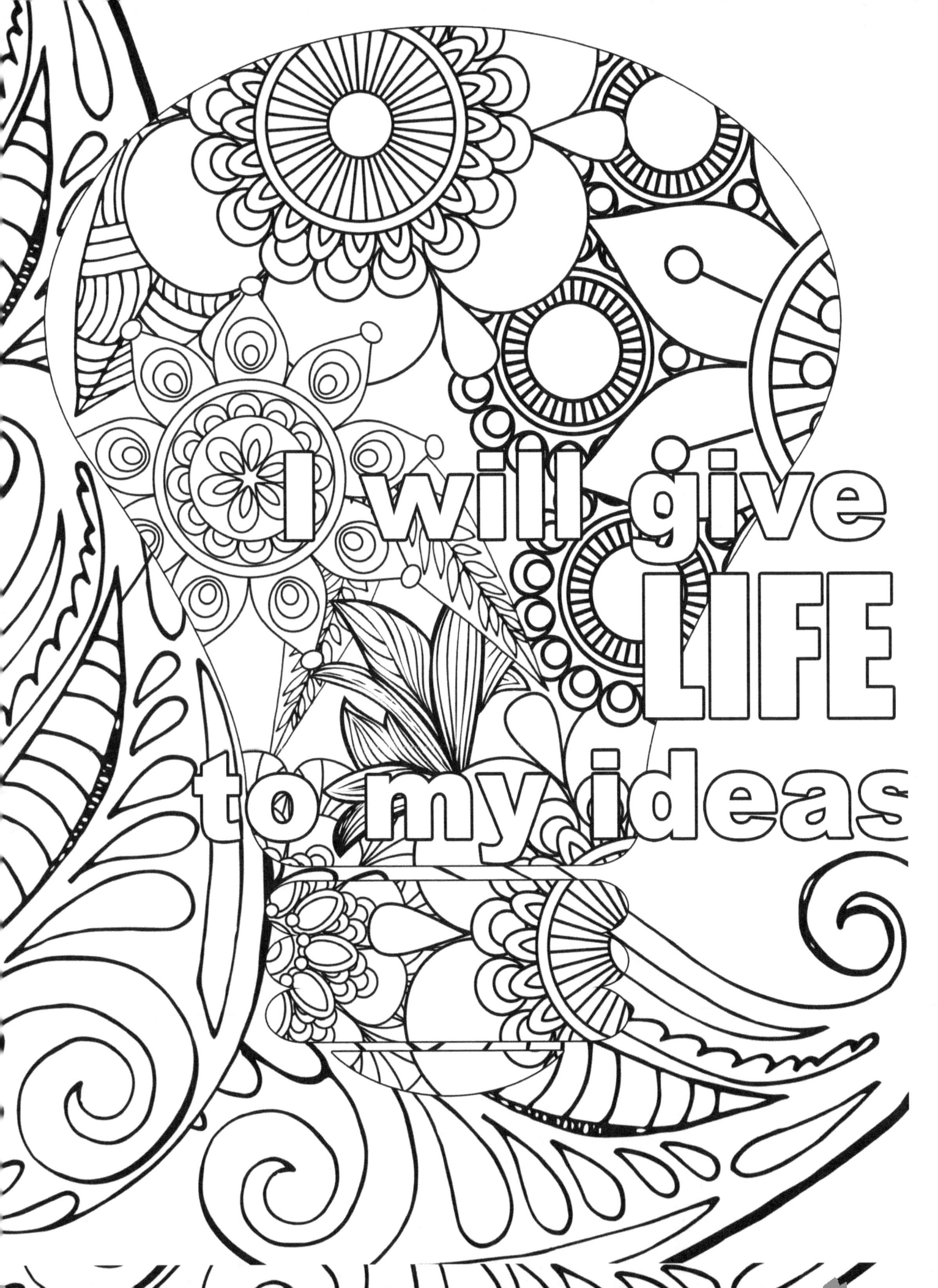

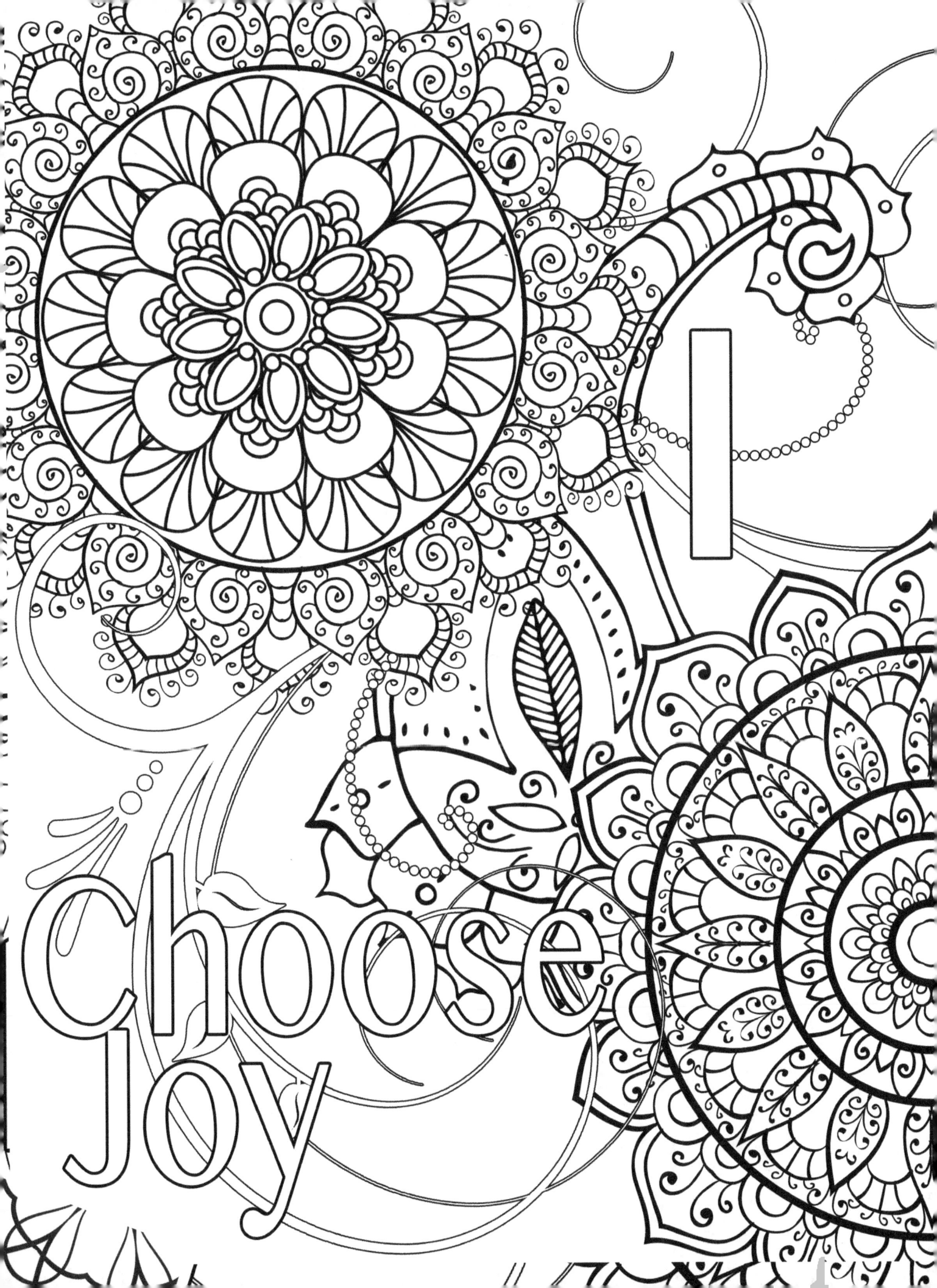

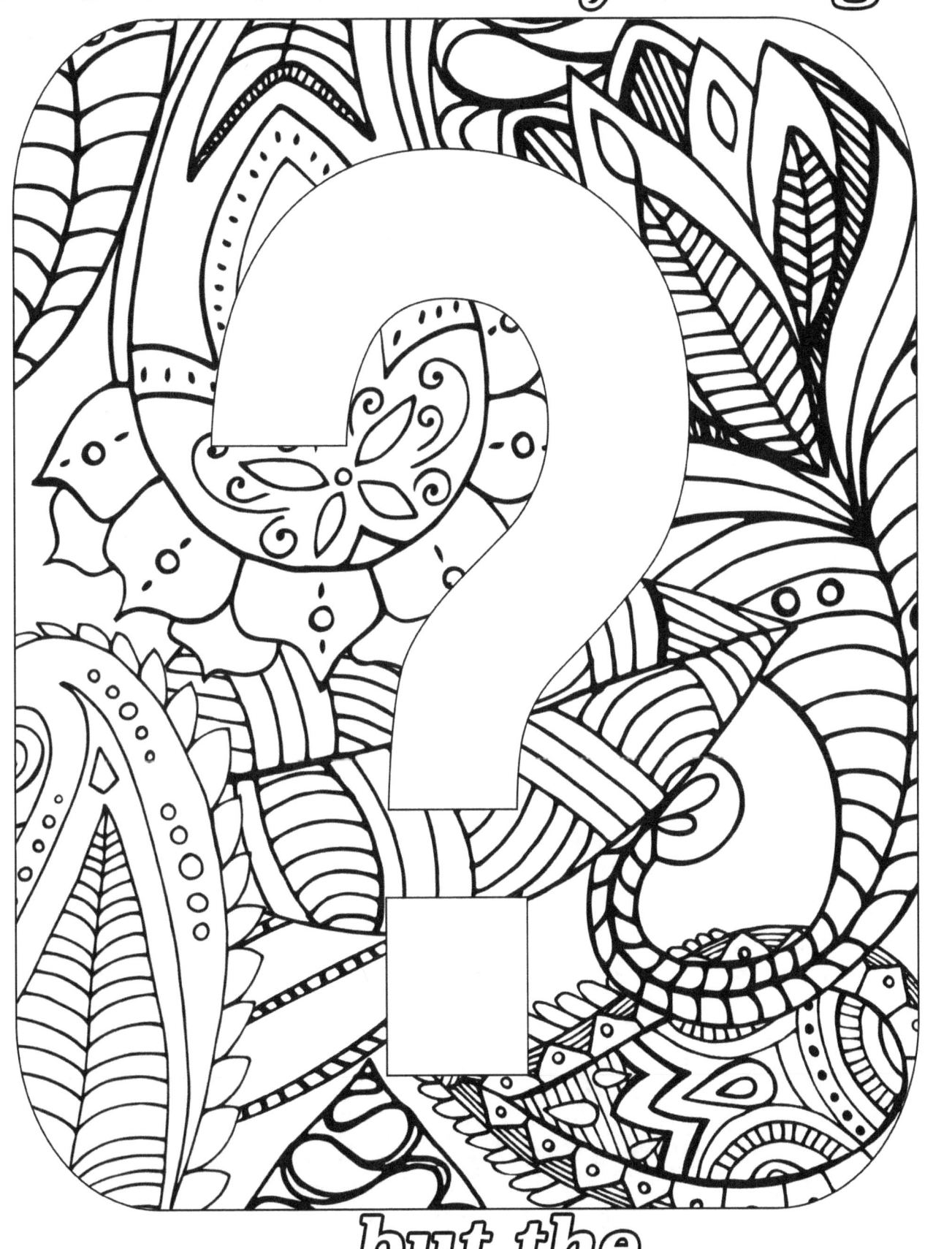

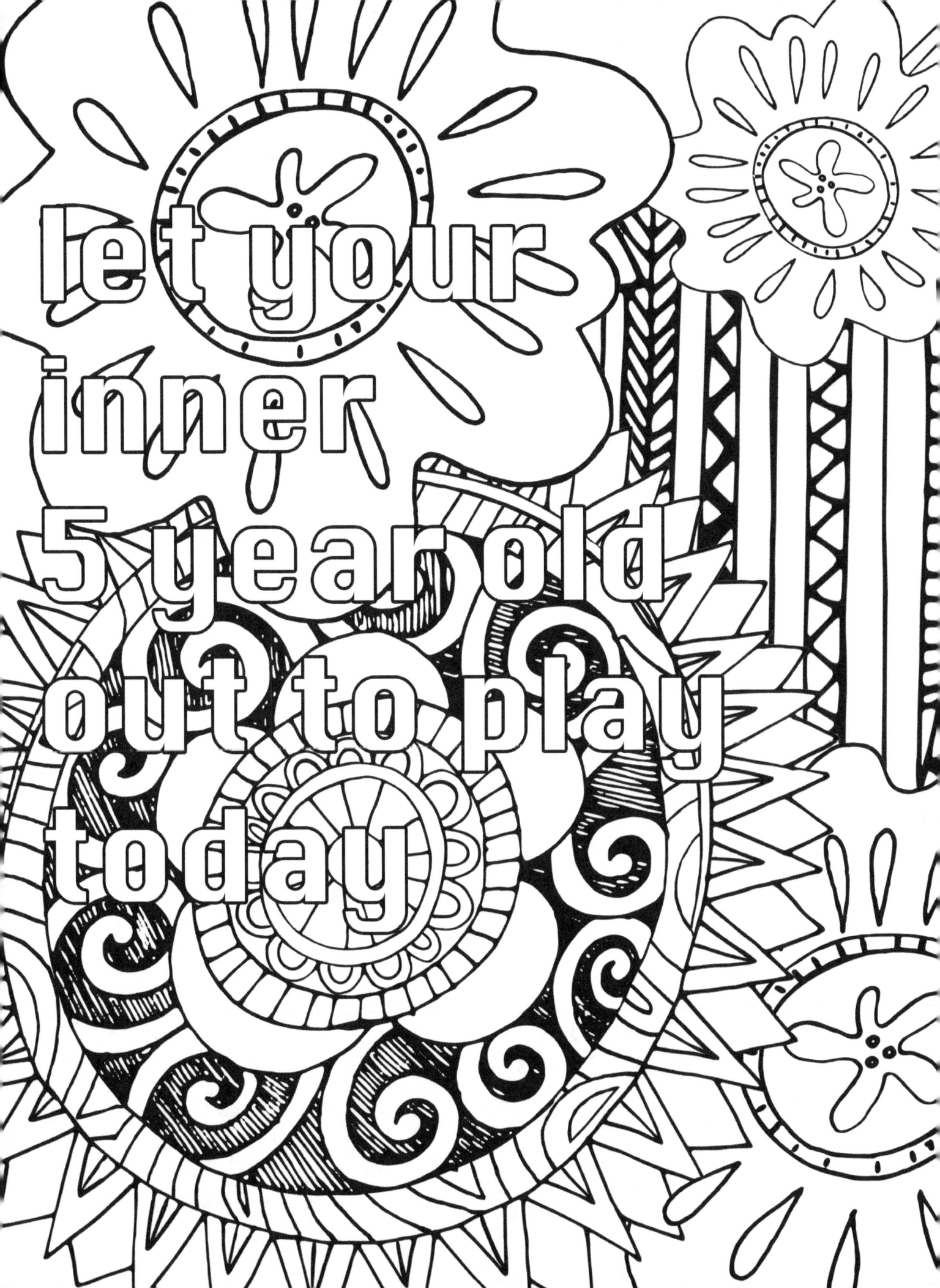

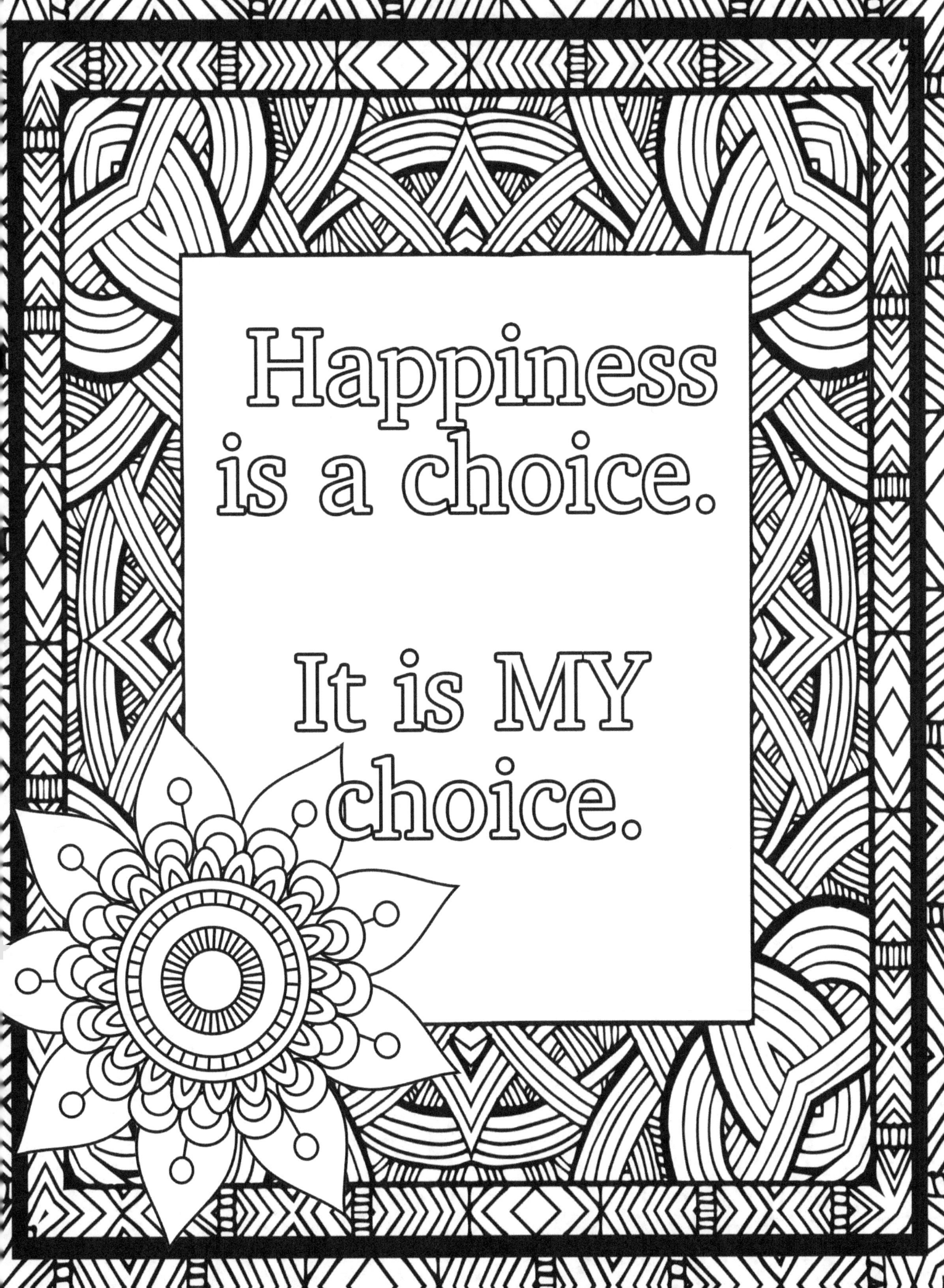

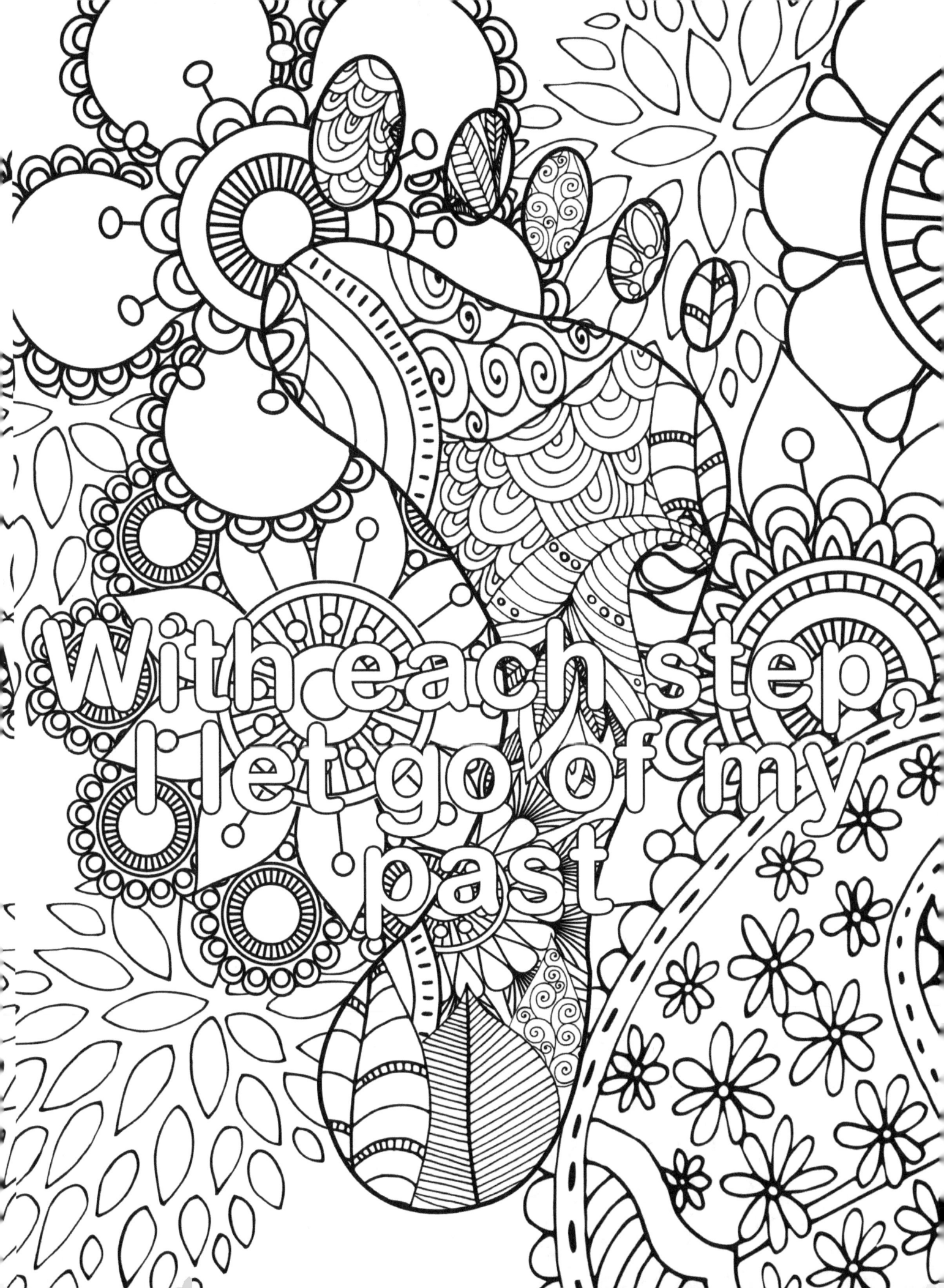

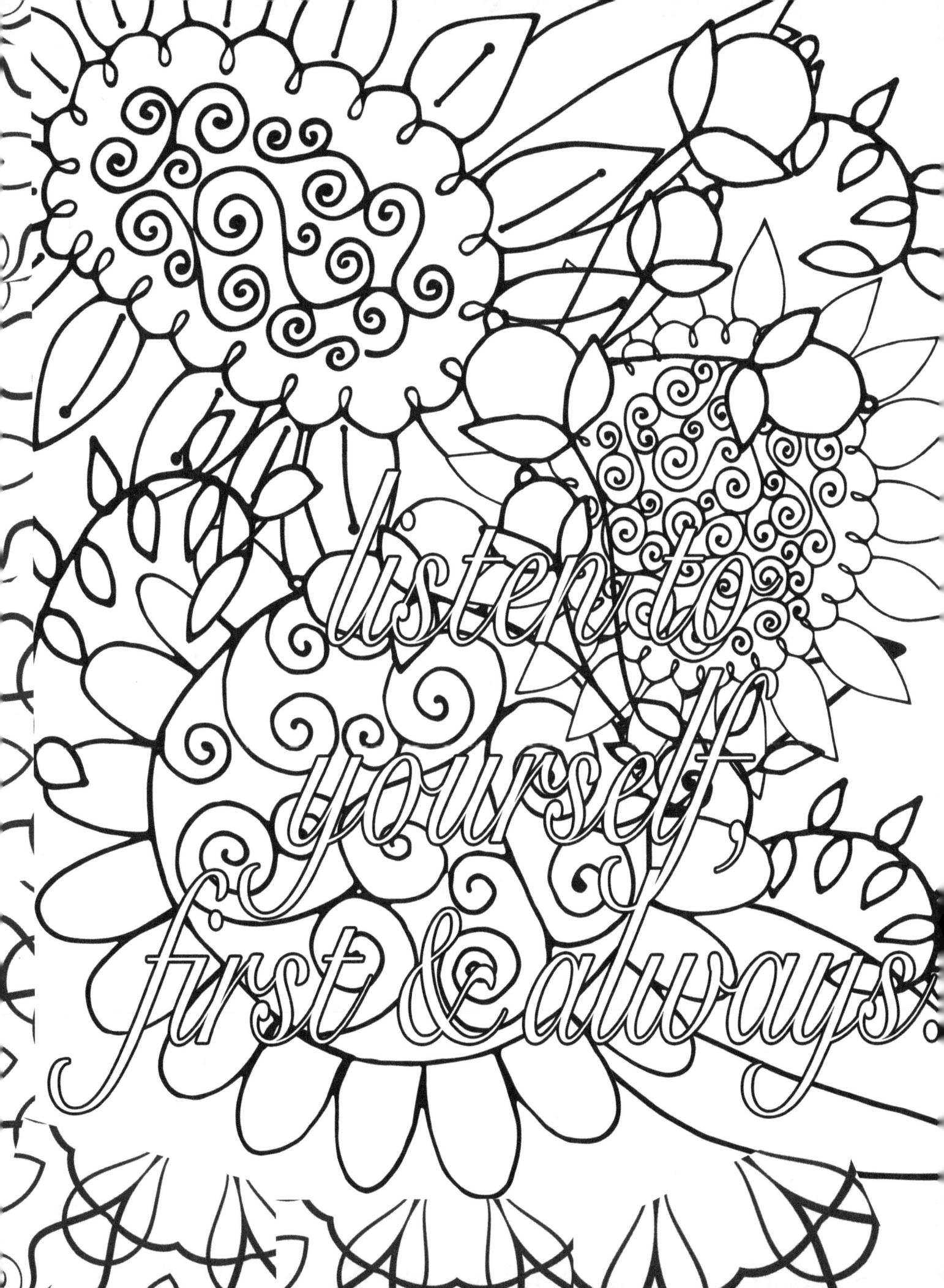

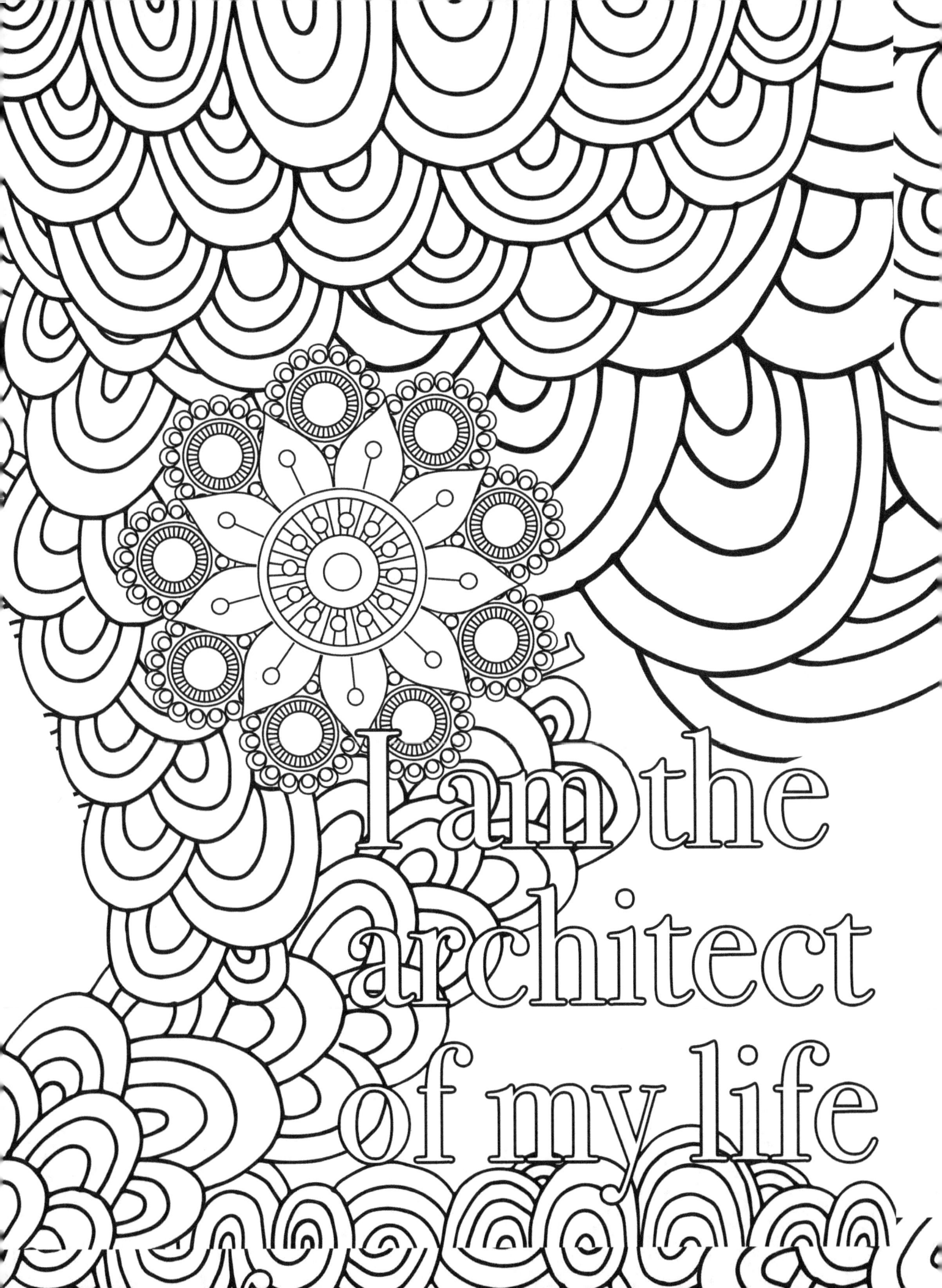

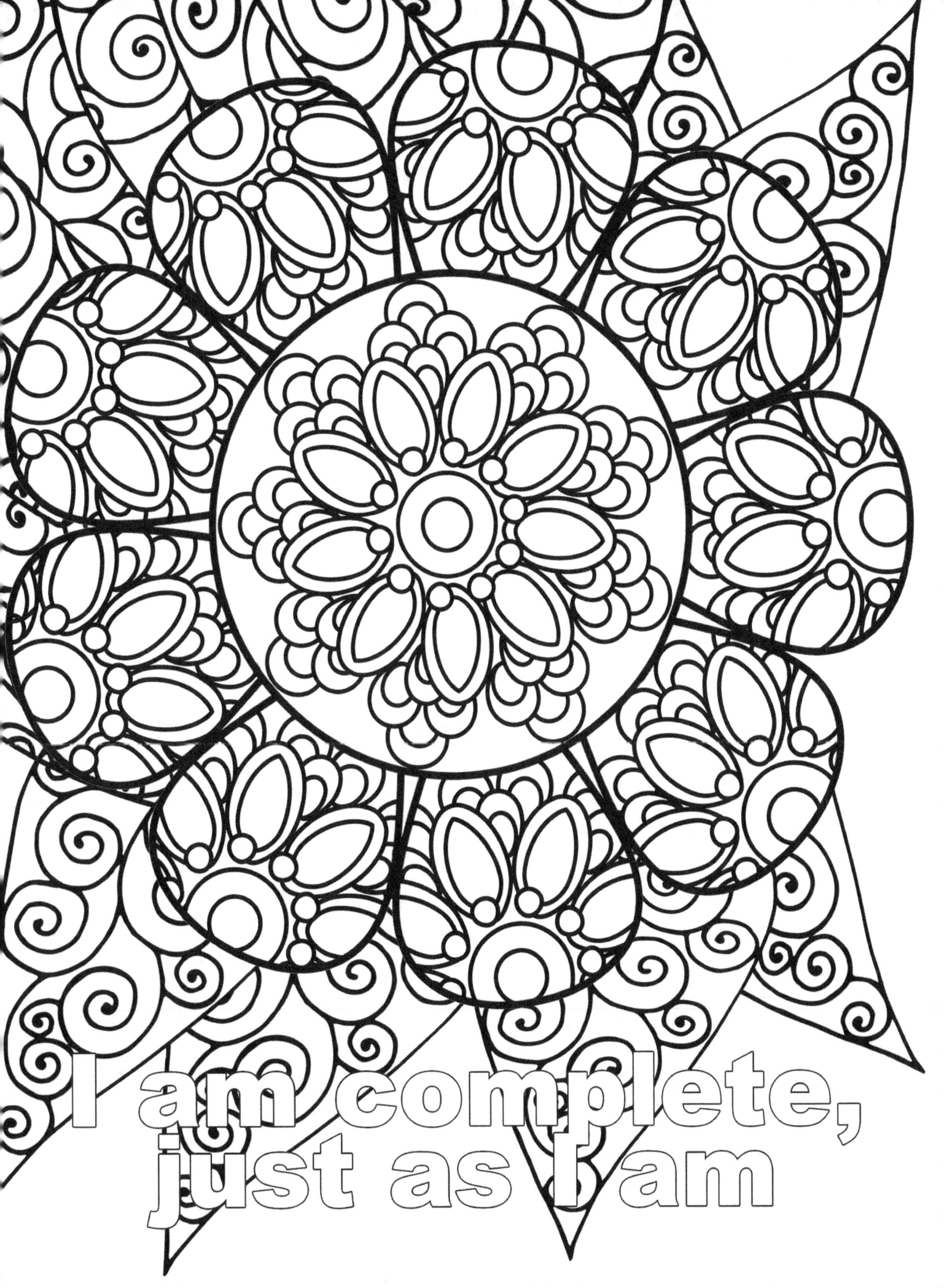

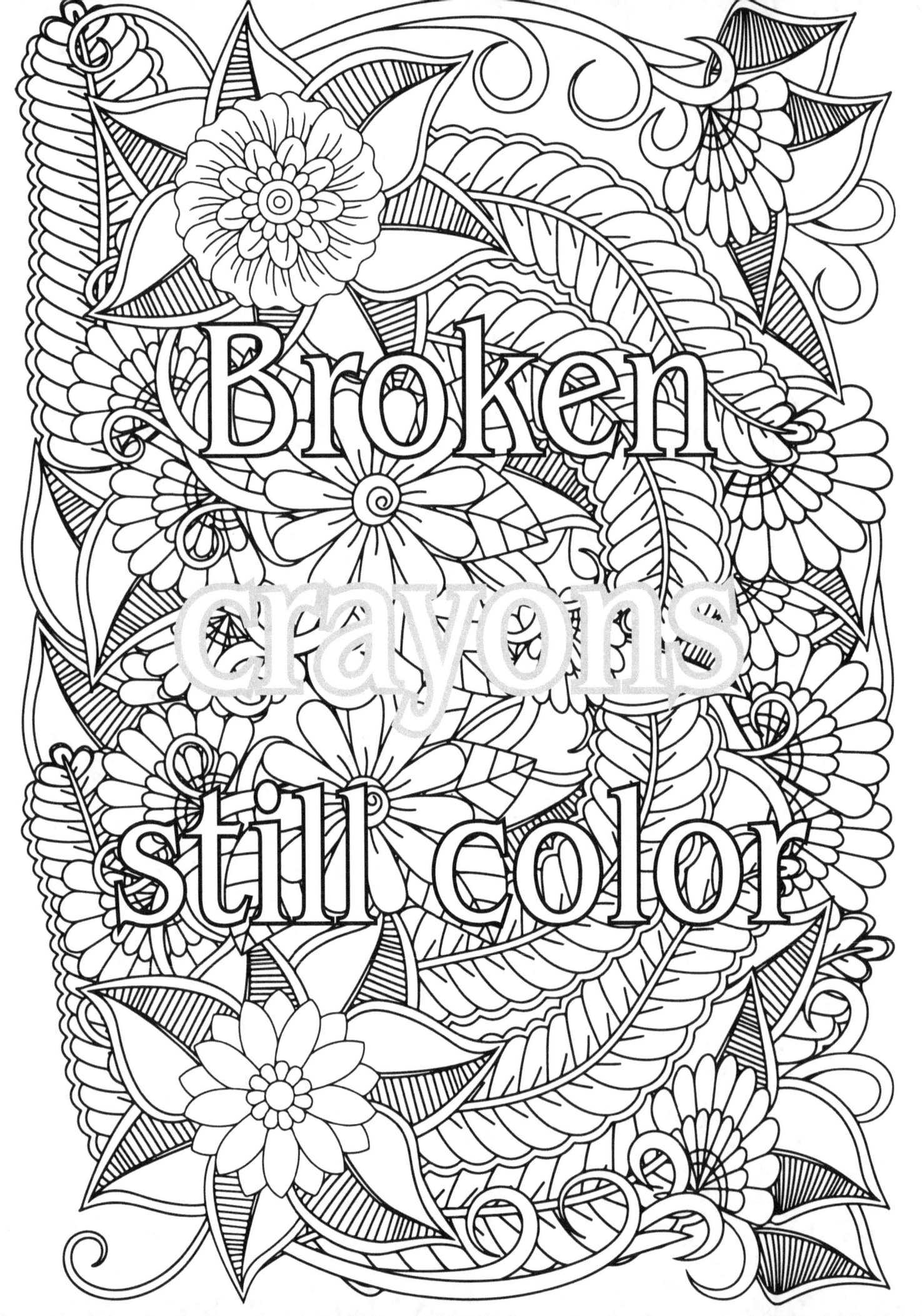

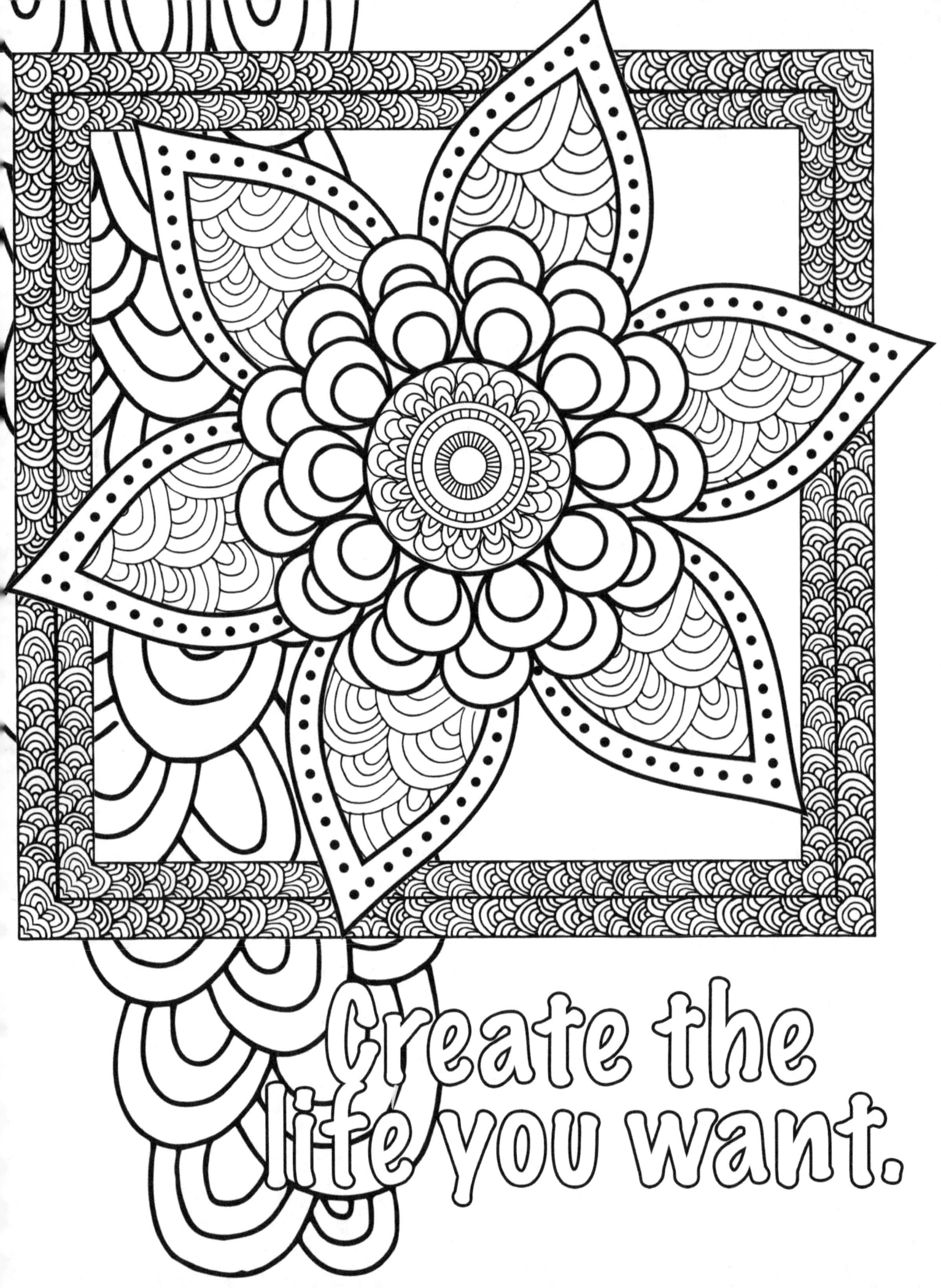

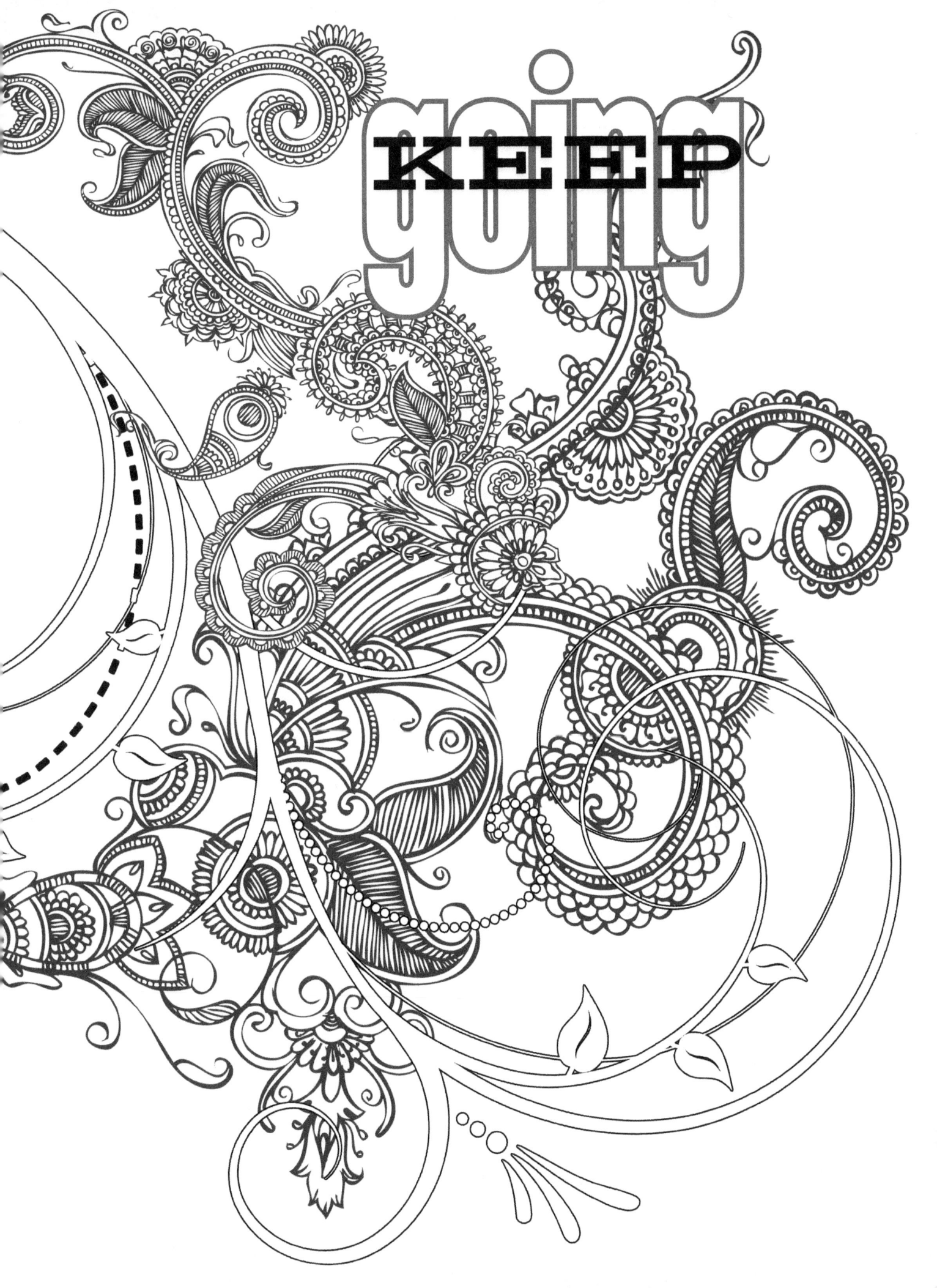

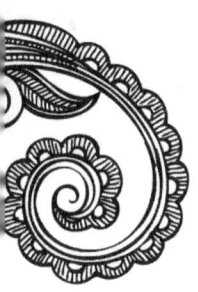

Colorful Farewell

As we bid farewell, we extend our heartfelt gratitude for joining us on this vibrant journey. Your support is deeply appreciated, and we feel honored to have been a part of your creative experience.

May each stroke of color bring you happiness, relaxation, and endless inspiration. Remember, in the world of art, there are no limits—only boundless opportunities to explore.

Wishing you abundant creativity, unfettered imagination, and countless moments of colorful bliss.

Thank you, and best wishes for your continued artistic endeavors!

Warm regards,

Harper Quinn

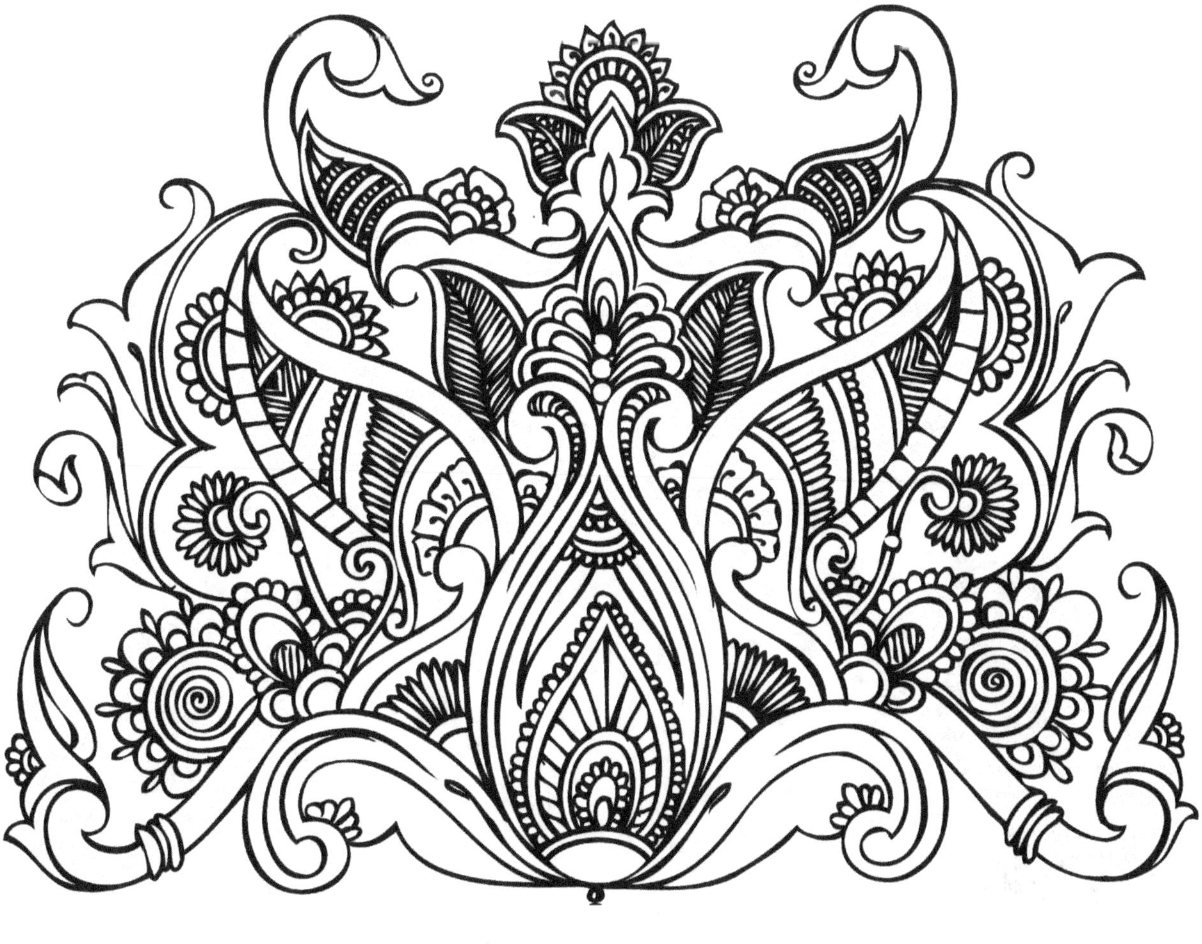

www.ingramcontent.com/pod-product-compliance
Lightning Source LLC
Chambersburg PA
CBHW082217220526
45470CB00010B/3203